SOME

HOLINESS

CORNERSTONES

ISBN 0-88019-293-3

By Richard S. Taylor

Schmul Publishing Co., Inc.
Wesleyan Book Club   1992   Salem, Ohio

Printed by
Old Paths Tract Society
Shoals, IN 47581

Foreword

Dr. Richard Taylor in this book has given us a clear, Biblical, scholarly view of some "holiness cornerstones." But he has done more. He has carefully and skillfully uncovered the foundations of our holiness faith.

Valuable in any age, such a volume as this is crucially significant in this day. It gives a clear sound on the trumpet in a time when Christians seem increasingly inclined to accommodate and to feel comfortable with sin.

How can we live a holy life? How can we be free of the "grip" as well as the guilt of sin? Dr. Taylor gives succinct, scriptural answers to these questions in this little volume.

There is something here for those steeped in the holiness message, for those somewhat familiar with it, and for those unacquainted or opposed to it. There is here a clear call to consider, to accept, and to experience God's provision for that "deeper walk" with Him.

Those of us at Wesley Biblical Seminary who heard the messages in October, 1990, were greatly helped by Dr. Taylor's fresh Presentation of the old, old story of God's sanctifying work in the life of the believer. Now we rejoice that a much wider audience will benefit from his exposition. Once you read this little volume you will no doubt want to share it with as many others as you can.

Harold G. Spann, LL.D.
President, Wesley Biblical Seminary
Jackson, Mississippi

Preface

With great joy Sir Wilfred Grenfell, medical missionary to the Labrador, took his new launch on its maiden voyage. It had been built in Liverpool, England for his use in reaching outlying villages. While seeking to follow the charts, he suddenly became aware that he was heading straight for the rocks. Later, when be disassembled the compass, he found that a careless workman, not having the proper brass screw handy, had substituted a steel screw in putting the compass together. The result was an unreliable compass, and near disaster.

The industrial and scientific world is full of anecdotal proofs that small errors can wreak great damage. This is as true theologically as mechanically and scientifically. Even those who build sincerely on the foundation Jesus Christ are in danger, Paul says, of building with "wood, hay, or straw," instead of "gold, silver, costly stones" (1 Cor. 3:12). The correctness of the foundation does not guarantee the soundness of the superstructure.

While this little book is by no means a systematic or comprehensive presentation of holiness theology—or an attempt to deal with all the "cornerstones"—it seeks to discuss helpfully some issues especially acute in the contemporary Wesleyan world. They can scarcely be viewed as minor matters of personal opinion. They bear too many major implications for that.

These five chapters were delivered as the 1990 Chamberlain Holiness Lectures at the Wesley Biblical Seminary in Jackson, Mississippi. The chapter on "Temptation and Sin" is an adaptation of a paper read to a section of the annual Evangelical Theological Society meeting held at Gordon-Conwell Theological Seminary, South Hamilton, Massachusetts, in 1987. Some of my Australian readers will recognize parts of Chapter

Five as derived and adapted from a similar lecture given at the Nazarene Bible College in Brisbane, 1984.

These chapters were prepared as papers to be heard, not read. Therefore the style is simpler and less formal than would be expected in scholarly papers for a theological journal. Every effort was made to be scholarly, but not forbiddingly so. I am really not as anxious for them to be read by classroom professionals as by the front line practioners, who need to be clear in what they teach and preach.

I hope I am not deluding myself in believing that the positions advocated in this little book are within the ballpark of mainline Wesleyanism, as represented not only by John Wesley and his peers, but by acknowledged holiness leaders of the 19th and 20th centuries. Yet I recognize that the very necessity of being polemical in my approach (primarily in chapters One and Three) is an acknowledgment that some variations of opinion can be found within contemporary Wesleyanism. I do not wish to reflect on the "Wesleyan credentials" of those who see some issues differently. Yet having said that, I must add that to me these issues are sufficiently major, and some deviations sufficiently critical, that I feel not only justified but bound to discuss them, as boldly (and I trust fairly) as I know how.

Yet I would not exaggerate the polemical content of these discussions. I would like to think that in the majority of these chapters some new ground is broken, and positions taken that will carry wide, if not unanimous, endorsement among us.

This Preface is a mix of figures—cornerstones, foundations, broken ground. Now let us add a fourth: trumpets. See Paul in 1 Corinthians 14:8 for what I mean. Perhaps an alternative title to this small volume could be, *Avoiding an Uncertain Trumpet.**

Richard S. Taylor
Bremerton, Washington, 1992

*Unless otherwise indicated, all Scripture quotations will be from the New American Standard Version (NASB).

Contents

CHAPTER ONE

Pentecost and Purity:
What Did Peter Mean in Acts 15:8-9?

"And God, who knows the heart, bore witness to them, giving them the Holy Spirit, just as he also did to us; and he made no distinction between us and them, cleansing their hearts by faith" (Acts 15:8-9).

The Holiness Movement has long believed that Acts 15:8-9 is a cornerstone passage for three doctrines: one, that the purifying of the heart is the heart of Pentecost; two, that the heart is cleansed by faith; and three, that this experience follows justification.

Typical is the statement by Russell R. Byrum: "The purification of heart to which Peter here refers evidently took place when he visited Cornelius. He states that God gave them the Spirit and purified their hearts. Doubtless that cleansing was that which we here designate sanctification and was subsequent to conversion. But the experience of Cornelius was normal in this respect, for Peter says God did to them 'even as he did unto us,' the apostles, at Pentecost in harmony with Jesus' prayer for their sanctification in John 17:17."[1]

In view of these deeply entrenched beliefs it may seem superfluous to reaffirm them. The problem is, all three doctrines have of recent years had their detractors within Wesleyan circles. In very subtle ways the positions have been undermined, especially as related to Acts 15:8-9. As an example of the approach: The secondness has been challenged, also the nature of the cleansing, by an argument based on the fact that "cleansing" is an aorist participle, and therefore should be interpreted as implying cleansing prior to the infilling of the Spirit.

That non-Wesleyans should espouse this is understandable. Phillips' paraphrase, for instance, says: "Moreover, God who knows men's inmost thoughts had plainly shown that this is so, for when he had cleansed their hearts through their faith he gave the Holy Spirit to the gentiles exactly as he did to us." The implication is that when they were justified by faith they were eligible for the fullness of the Holy Spirit. That this is true doctrine we concede; in fact it is basic to holiness theology. But that this is all Peter meant by the word "cleansing" as used in this context is the cornerstone issue.

Perhaps it is time therefore to take a fresh look at this passage. Our inquiry will be twofold: First, we will reexamine the *timing* and the *nature* of heart purity. This will be our focus in this chapter. In the second chapter we will seek to grasp what Peter meant by attaching heart cleansing to faith.

Timing—Prior or Together?

In respect to the purifying of the heart, the question of timing can be disposed of first. It is true that the word for cleansing, *katharisas* (from *katharidzō*), as an aorist participle, is dependent on the main verb of v. 9a, *outhen diekrinen*, "made no distinction," and could therefore be translated "having purified," since normally the action of an aorist participle is prior to the action of the verb on which it leans. But the conclusion that therefore the passage declares a heart cleansing before the outpouring of the Spirit is a bit hasty, because its coordinate participle, *dous*, "giving" is also aorist. This is dependent on the coordinate verb, *emarturēsen*, "bore witness," and could be translated "having given." If we feel compelled to handle one aorist participle in the customary way, there is no good reason why we should not handle the other participle in that way also. Let us see how the passage will read if we thus render both aorist participles: "And God, who knows the heart, bore witness to them, having given them the Holy Spirit, just as He also did to us; and He made no distinction between us and them, having cleansed their hearts by faith." Reading it this way makes it clear that the cleansing of the heart and the giving of the Holy Spirit are still simultaneous. Therefore, the exegesis of purifying as being prior to the infilling with the Spirit breaks down.

Probably the identical parsing of these two participles and their attachment to coordinate verbs explains why by far the majority of translators assume that in this case they imply simultaneous action instead of successive. The NEB, for instance, renders the passage: "And God, who can read men's minds, showed his approval of them by giving the Holy Spirit to them, as he did to us. He made no difference between them and us; for he purified their hearts by faith." We conclude therefore that there is no sufficient exegetical reason for separating the cleansing from the baptism with the Holy Spirit. On the contrary the strong implication is that they belong together as two aspects of one experience.

What the Cleansing was Not

Having dealt with the issue of timing, let us now consider the meaning of *katharisas tas kardias auton*, "purifying their hearts."

The bedrock premise. Our attempt to determine this will be gravely if not fatally flawed if we do not first acknowledge a basic premise in Peter's mind. *He is very pointedly declaring that whatever Cornelius and his household experienced was precisely what the apostles and other believers had experienced at Pentecost.* Theologically, this is not just a cornerstone; it is bedrock.

This is not the first time Peter has emphasized this. When defending his action in going to the Gentiles some time before, he reported, "And as I began to speak, the Holy Spirit fell upon them, just as He did upon us at the beginning. And I remembered the word of the Lord, how He used to say, 'John baptized with water, but you shall be baptized with the Holy Spirit.' If

God therefore gave to them the same gift as He gave to us also after believing in the Lord Jesus Christ, who was I that I could stand in God's way?" (Acts 11:15-17).

The similarity between that explanatory statement and the one before us is striking. What happened in both events is thus identified by Peter as the baptism with the Holy Spirit. The nature of the gift or bestowment was the same; and significantly (in the light of the discussion on timing above), Peter declares the experience as *subsequent* to "believing in the Lord Jesus Christ."[2] While heart cleansing does not precede the baptism with the Spirit, believing unto salvation does.

What stands out in Peter's mind in the Acts 15 discussion was the effect the baptism with the Spirit had on the heart: *it was purified*. It is this declaration which brings his argument into direct contact with the issue before them in this first major church council. The watershed importance of this will become more clear as we proceed.

In the meanwhile, if we are to understand the meaning of heart cleansing we must keep reminding ourselves that whatever it meant for Cornelius and his circle was identical to what it meant for the 120 who tarried in the Upper Room. This too is bedrock.

What Must be Ruled Out. When we study what God did for the apostles and others on the Day of Pentecost we will be compelled to rule out two possible meanings in the use of the word *katharisas*. These two possible meanings are ceremonial cleansing and expiatory cleansing.

1. We confront the word *katharizo* used in its ceremonial sense in the prelude to Peter's trip to Caesarea. When Peter protested eating the creatures he saw in his vision God answered, "What God has cleansed, no longer consider unholy" (Acts 10:15). After the third time Peter finally got the message, and when he reached the house of Cornelius he interpreted it splendidly: "God has shown me that I should not call any man unholy or unclean" (10:28). Was he saying that all men were

saved and sanctified? Obviously not. He now understood that God had cleansed the Gentiles in the sense that the wall of separation between Jew and Gentile was declared invalid, and no longer to be an obstacle to the full evangelization of the Gentiles. Jews and Gentiles were equally the objects of Christ's redemptive provision.

The declaring of the Gentiles as acceptable before God, and therefore no longer off limits to Peter, brought to Peter a radical explosion of understanding respecting the scope of the gospel. But he also knew that such a "cleansing" was not in any sense the cleansing of forgiveness or the cleansing of sanctification; rather, to these blessings the Gentiles were now declared to have free and equal access.

But on still more fundamental grounds, such a sense of cleansing is ruled out of Peter's intended meaning in Acts 15:8-9, namely, by the simple fact that the Jewish believers at Pentecost had never needed such a ceremonial cleansing. They were already Israelites.

2. We confront the word *katharizō* in its *expiatory* sense in Ephesians 5:25. Here the NASB is our most reliable guide, for it gives full force to the aorist participle, which in this case makes abundant sense when given its normal meaning of antecedent action. It reads: "Husbands, love your wives, just as Christ also loved the church and gave Himself up for her; that He might sanctify her, *having cleansed* her by the washing of water with the word" (italics added). The parallel of this with the phrase in Titus 3:5, "the washing of regeneration," seems unmistakable (cf. Acts 22:16). The cleansing symbolized by water is the washing of John the Baptist's cleansing, forgiveness of sins. This is the cleansing of expiation, which the NASB declares to be *prerequisite* to Christ's further sanctifying work.

This is confirmed by relating the "washing of water" kind of cleansing to John the Baptist's teaching. His baptism, he said, was the water baptism, and was the mark of repentance and the forgiveness of sins; i.e., the cleansing of expiation. But he pointed to a future baptism to be administered by Jesus which he called the baptism with the Holy Spirit and fire. The baptism with the Spirit is not a water baptism, but a fire baptism; and fire speaks of a deeper kind of cleansing than water denotes.

Now, how does this relate to the first Pentecost in Jerusalem and the Gentile Pentecost in Caesarea?

Respecting Cornelius the data is admittedly a little hazy. Reams of paper have been devoted to the debate over exactly when Cornelius entered into a justified relationship to Christ. The Calvinists, and some Wesleyans, solve the problem by seeing Cornelius as a case of simultaneous new birth and Spirit baptism. But the facts which are available to us do not require such a conclusion.

Let us keep the facts before us. Cornelius was a lover of the true God, was a man of prayer, and a man of good works. Moreover, according to Peter he was by no means unacquainted with the story of Christ. That at some point he touched God for assurance of the forgiveness of sins is strongly implied in Peter's phrasing, "And God, who knows the heart, bore witness to them;" i.e., in the act of pouring out the Holy Spirit upon this man and his circle God was bearing witness to them that their hearts were ready. The *readiness* of v. 8 is the preparedness of the heart for the *cleansing* of v. 9. Nowhere is there a clear instance of the sanctifying gift of the Spirit upon unforgiven and unregenerate persons. This observation would lend endorsement to the position of Ralph Earle as being eminently sensible. He says:

> Perhaps the explanation which best accords with Scripture is that while Peter was only getting well started with his sermon . . . his hearers in their hearts believed on Jesus Christ and experienced evangelical conversion—as did John Wesley while sitting in a society meeting on Aldersgate Street. . . . Then, because their hearts were fully open for all of

God's will, these listeners who had walked devoutly in the light of Judaism (10:2), and had now accepted Christ, were suddenly filled with the Holy Spirit. This reconstruction of what took place does not ignore or suppress any statements in the biblical account.[3]

But even if some remain dubious about Cornelius and his circle the case with the apostles is completely unambiguous. The heart cleansing they received at Pentecost could not have been the cleansing of expiation. That they had experienced forgiveness—probably under John's ministry—and were regenerate persons, is a position so unassailable that it seems futile to take the time here to review the evidence. According to Jesus their names were written in heaven (Luke 10:20). They were not of the world, even as Jesus was not of the world (John 17:14). They were clean through the word Jesus had given them (John 15:3). They were branches in Christ the vine (v. 5). And so we could go on, but surely such an exercise would be needless. The conclusion remains that the purifying of the heart that Peter was thinking of, which occurred in the hearts of the apostles on the Day of Pentecost and which occurred in the household of Cornelius, could not have been either a ceremonial *katharismos* or an expiatory *katharismos* but something else, and obviously, something deeper.

The Nature of the Cleansing

The delineation of this deeper cleansing can be made in three ways:

1. *First,* we can remind ourselves that what Peter is talking about is a cleansing of the *heart*. This is simply loaded with significance. Here is not a cleansing of the *record*: that is forgiveness. Neither is it a cleansing even of the *life*: that is a fruit of repentance and regeneration. It is a cleansing of the heart, and this surely denotes the hidden springs of the moral and spiritual nature. That in the heart which needs to be cleansed

is whatever James meant by double-mindedness: "Cleanse your hands you sinners, and purify your hearts, you double-minded" (Jas. 4:8). It is what Jesus had in mind when He saw the human heart as the fountainhead of all wickedness: "For from within, out of the heart of men, proceed evil thoughts," and the vile flow of sin which stains the human race (Mark 7:21-23). It is whatever that twist and perversity is that prompted Jeremiah to diagnose the heart as "more deceitful than all else" and "desperately sick" (Jer.17:9).

It is clear that in the heart is a profound corruption, that which Paul calls the principle or law of indwelling sin (Rom. 7), which cries out for an incisive and equally profound purging. In the Christian this corruption does not reign, but nevertheless compromises the soul as a residue of self-sovereignty, an egoism not yet broken, a root of bitterness and unbelief, which deprives of power and shackles the spiritual life.

A purified heart can only be what Jesus had in mind in the beatitude, "Blessed are the pure in heart, for they shall see God" (Matt. 5:8).

2. The *second* way open to us for delineating the inner substance of that in the heart which needs cleansing is to look at the apostles. According to Peter they experienced this deeper cleansing when baptized with the Holy Spirit. How did this cleansing affect them? How did the change in them pinpoint the nature of the problem?

Surely it is obvious to any careful reader of the New Testament that the really magnificent miracle of Pentecost, beside which the wind and tongues were not only incidental but almost insignificant, was the transformation in these eleven men. They had been with Jesus for some three years, day in and day out; but too little had penetrated the thick hide of their carnality. They were prize egotists. They loved Jesus, believed that He was the Son of God, and had forsaken all to follow Him—but never stopped angling for position and advantage. They dreamed daily of power and grandeur. Their love was thoroughly mixed with self-serving, of the crassest kind. They continually displayed an endemic spiritual dullness, which never did break out of the narrow, provincial bonds of earthiness and make them capable of really experiencing the beatific vision. Even at the Passover with Christ they were still quarreling among themselves over rank. After the resurrection, Peter, who had been mercifully forgiven his shameful denial, and now mercifully commissioned, right there had a burst of jealousy toward John.

But when filled with the Spirit the contrast between their sudden spiritual-mindedness and their former carnal-mindedness; their new selflessness and their former self-centeredness; their courage in contrast to their cowardice; and most amazing of all, the thorough internalization of their discipleship, would be hard to believe if we didn't see the evidence spread across the pages of Acts and the Epistles.

There is no escape from the conclusion that underlying these incredible outward changes was a profound inner change, a change so radical and so deep that we are compelled to see it as a restructuring of their very nature. It was an alteration which made them Christ-centered in a new way, and which turned the grain of their nature to the grain of God's holiness and God's perfect will for them. Selfish ambition was totally gone. Jockeying for position was history, jealousy and envy never again raised their ugly heads. Their hearts were cleansed. And for all time this sets the flag for any sound doctrine of Pentecost.

The Circumcision Crux

But there is a third method of determining the inner essence of this heart cleansing. It is to remind ourselves of the issue that Peter and the others were debating: whether or not the Gentile believers should be required to be circumcised and keep the law of Moses. That was the burning question which brought them together. The story is graphically related in the context. Some of the believing Pharisees wanted Jesus without giving up Moses; most of all they wanted to protect the insular uniqueness of the Jewish claim to be God's chosen people, and perpetuate the long-standing principle that if you were to benefit by God's covenant with Israel you must put yourself within the Jewish fold. And this was impossible without male circumcision. So they had marched off to Antioch, where there was a swelling tide of Gentile conversions, and announced: "Unless you are circumcised, according to the custom taught by Moses, you cannot be saved." Christ alone cannot save; it must be Christ plus Moses, and the badge of the Jewish covenant is circumcision.

This was what prompted this first general church council, and what Peter was debating. His argument was more decisive than even that of Paul and Barnabas, who spoke first. They could argue that the marks of true *regeneration* were already incontrovertible in the Antiochian Christians. But Peter's account brought the case to the very heart of the whole circumcision question. For he recounted the experience of the Gentile Cornelius and his Gentile circle who not only were converted to Christ but baptized with the Holy Spirit, and in the process experienced what *circumcision had always pointed to, the purifying of the heart.* Peter therefore is saying, "They already have what circumcision stands for; and God has already witnessed to the fact that He is pleased with them. Why then insult God by imposing a requirement which God has not imposed?" Why call for the shadow when you have the substance? Why impose a type when you have the antitype? Why insist on putting an arm in a cast when the arm is already healed?

At this point it is necessary to pin down our thesis, which is that circumcision really did prefigure holiness of heart, and that it implied secondness, that is, a work of grace done on God's justified people. Paul indirectly implies secondness when he reminds the Roman Christians that Abraham was justified by faith before the rite of circumcision was given (Rom. 4:10). As a matter of history, the institution was given at Abraham's second major spiritual crisis, when God changed his name and called him to perfection, or blamelessness (Gen. 17:1-11).

It is true that Paul immediately in Rom. 4:11 connects the rite of circumcision with justification by faith, as a sign and a seal. But he also declared a deeper meaning in Colossians—a passage which will claim our attention shortly.

As for the implied holiness metaphor Laurence W. Wood points out that circumcision even before Abraham was well known as a type of purity.[4] In this case the children of Israel would have understood from the start the meaning of the rite. This would explain why Moses could so naturally use the term in Deuteronomy 10:16 and 30:6 in the way he did. In 10:16 he gives a command, "Circumcise then your heart," and in 30:6 a promise: "Moreover the LORD your God will circumcise your heart and the heart of your descendants, to love the LORD your God with all your heart and with all your soul, in order that you may live." Wood points out that the Septuagint actually substitutes in this passage the word "cleanse" for "circumcise."[5] In other words, for the translators of the original Hebrew into Greek, circumcision and cleansing were synonymous.

But the fulfillment of God's promise to circumcise their hearts was still waiting, for the Sanhedrin, Judaism's flower of religious culture, had not yet experienced it. The martyr-deacon Stephen, in his epochal sermon, pierced and enraged them with his indictment: "You men who are stiffnecked and uncircumcised in heart and ears are always resisting the Holy Spirit; you are doing just as your fathers did" (Acts 7:51). These men had been circumcised in body, but what that circumcision prefigured was still alien to them. Now Peter is announcing that the fulfillment is to be found through Jesus, in His baptism with the Holy Spirit. And Paul concurs by saying that the only circumcision which really matters is that "which is of the heart, by the Spirit, not by the letter" (Rom. 2:29).

Our squeamish delicacy in handling this subject must not be allowed to obscure the blunt reality here. We are dealing with a term that has in it the meaning of an inherited abnormality of the soul which needs to be excised. Jeremiah does not sidestep the graphic metaphor when he declares the Lord's message to Israel:

> "Circumcise yourselves to the LORD
> And remove the foreskins of your heart" (Jer. 4:4).

The carnal nature is an inherited excess of egoism, a bent to self-centeredness, an abnormality in the affectional and volitional propensities, which needs the knife of the sanctifying Holy Spirit, and will yield to no other knife.[7]

Both the timing and the nature of this circumcision is stated so clearly by Paul in Colossians 2:11-13 that it is amazing there should be any cavil about the essence of heart cleansing. We get the picture better by noting v. 13 first: "And when you were dead in your sins and in the uncircumcision of your sinful nature, God made you alive with Christ" (NIV). Here are two problems: guilt and an uncircumcised nature. Now notice how Paul handles the double cure in vv. 11-12: "In Him you were also circumcised, in the putting off of the sinful nature, not with a circumcision done by the hands of men but with the circumcision done by Christ, *having been* buried with him in baptism and raised with him through your faith in the power of God" (NIV, italics added). Not "being buried" but "having been." Our burial with Christ in baptism precedes our spiritual circumcision.

Now the inspired apostle is not getting his metaphors mixed. He is writing with exact precision. Baptism is not the New Testament counterpart of Old Testament circumcision. Baptism as a water rite is a sign of birth which precedes circumcision. The New Testament counterpart to circumcision is Pentecost, reenacted in each experience of being baptized with the Holy Spirit, whether the 120 or Cornelius or Christians today.

We have every reason to conclude therefore that the purification of the heart experienced in the baptism with the Holy Spirit consists of the radical removal of the inbred or original sin which lingers in the regenerate, and which is elsewhere called, the *sarx*, or "flesh," "the sinful nature" (NIV), "the sin that dwelleth in me," "the body of this death," the "law of sin and death," and "the mind set on the flesh."

"Who will set me free from the body of this death?" exclaims Paul in Romans 7:24. The answer is clear and exultant: "Thanks be to God through Jesus Christ our Lord!" (v. 25).

The practicality of this answer in experience can be vouched for by Grace Dawson. She gives her testimony in her remarkable little book, *Set Among Princes*. For years she rose no higher in her Christian life than what she had been taught to expect. She says: "There were frequent grievings of God by such sins as lack of true Christian love, resentments, outbursts of impatience, touchiness, and so on, causing friction with others. There was daily sinning, repenting, confessing to God and receiving His fresh forgiveness. On and on, month by month, year by year, it was a constant round of sinning, repenting, forgiveness, interspersed of course with some glad victories."

When she became desperate for something better she began to examine her inner life more closely. "I was shocked by what I discovered," she writes. "There was a great big *I* hidden in the depths of my personality which dominated everything. *I* was not appreciated. *I* had done so much for so-and-so and what thanks did *I* get? *My* opinions were disregarded. Why should *I* be told what to do? The way *I* was ignored and slighted! Terrible! Why shouldn't *I* remain quiet and aloof after such treatment? *I* must justify *myself* after such misrepresentation. Why do not *I* receive more consideration? *I* deserve it. *I*, *I*, *I*—ad infinitum! It was most humbling to discover how full of self I was. And the pride! I loathed it!"

Then one day a friend said: "Oh! your trouble is indwelling sin. You need to let Christ deal with that by filling you with His Spirit." In her account she says: "It hit me like a bombshell." But it led to a depth of prayer, Bible searching and holiness reading which finally opened her mind and heart to the truth. One day she touched God in His sanctifying grace and became a thoroughly emancipated woman—delivered from herself. This writer can bear personal witness to the radiance, depth, compassion, and steadiness that marked her from that day on.[8]

ENDNOTES

1. *Christian Theology* (Anderson, IN: Warner Press, rev. 1982; original date, 1925), p. 378. W. T. Purkiser says: "The enduring importance of Peter's testimony lies in his clear identification of the effect of Pentecost as purifying or cleansing (RSV) the hearts of those 'upon' whom the Holy Spirit comes. The phenomenon of speaking in other languages which occurred in Caesarea (10:46) as it had in Jerusalem is completely ignored by Peter. . . . For Peter, 20 years after Pentecost, the essential identification of the baptism or filling with the Holy Spirit is purity of heart" (*Exploring Christian Holiness* [Kansas City, MO: Beacon Hill Press of Kansas City, 1983], vol. 1, p. 124.) See also Daniel Steele, Benjamin Field, S. J. Gamertsfelder, H. Orton Wiley, et al., as cited in Richard S. Taylor, *Great Holiness Classics*, vol. 3, "Leading Wesleyan Thinkers" (Kansas City, MO: Beacon Hill Press of Kansas City, 1985). Gamertsfelder calls the understanding being defended as "the teaching of the primitive church" (GHC, p. 330).

2. The NASB brings this time sequence out very clearly; the NIV ignores it.

3. *Beacon Bible Commentary*, vol. 7, p. 383.

4. *Pentecostal Grace*, (Wilmore, KY: Francis Asbury Publishing Company, Inc. 1980), p. 138.

5. Ibid., p. 142. The scholarly support Wood marshalls for the connection of circumcision with holiness, and its symbolic meaning and promise in the Scriptures, is amazingly broad and convincing. See pp. 137ff.

To thus see circumcision is to see in it a lynchpin to the doctrine that entire sanctification is a "definite work of grace." Circumcision is an operation performed by one person upon another. Likewise entire sanctification is the decisive and crucial action of God (1 Thess. 5:23) upon His believing children—truly a "work" of grace.

6. Wesley concedes that in a very real sense the conflict described in Romans 7 is carried over into the regenerate life. While he affirms that the picture is primarily that of one under the law he proceeds to so qualify this as virtually to annul it. He says: "There does still *remain*, even in them that are justified, a *mind* which is in some measure *carnal*; (so the Apostle tells even the believers at Corinth, 'Ye are carnal;') an *heart bent to backsliding*, still ever ready to 'depart from the living God;' a propensity to pride, self-will, anger, revenge, love of the world, yea, and all evil; a root of bitterness, which, if the restraint were taken off for a moment, would instantly spring up; yes, such a depth of corruption, as, without clear light from God, we cannot possibly conceive. And a conviction of all this *remaining* in *their hearts* is the repentance which belongs to them that are justified" (*Works*, Vol. 5, p. 161).

7. For this to be affirmed as the intended theological meaning of the rite of circumcision, it is not necessary to prove an exact physiological parallel. In other words, the purification meaning is not dependent on demonstrating that the prepuce of uncircumcised males is an unhygienic abnormality. Medical opinion is divided on this issue.

8. *Set Among Princes: The Royal Road to Spiritual Riches* (Kansas City, MO: Beacon Hill Press of Kansas City, 1979), pp. 48-51.

CHAPTER TWO

Holiness and Faith:

How Does Sanctifying Faith Work?

Exercising faith for entire sanctification seems much more difficult than exercising faith for justification. In respect to justification we know that Christ's blood made atonement for our sins, and on the basis of that atonement we are encouraged to accept forgiveness by simple faith; and because we believe God's word is true, we do. Reaching out our hand and taking what is being offered to us is simple. If we have confidence in the giver, believing for the gift is almost without effort.

But the condition needing the work of grace we call entire sanctification is a profoundly ingrained state of our very soul. It is relatively easy to believe that I can be forgiven for what I have *done*; but to believe that I—yes, I—can be changed in my inmost being, so thoroughly that my disposition is altered, and my spontaneous affinities will be transformed, is a prospect which prompts a high degree of doubt, fear, and skepticism.

When I look at the change which has already occurred in my regeneration, I should realize that the alteration which we call sanctification has already been well started; therefore I ought not to doubt God's ability to finish what He has begun. Nevertheless, when Christians become aware of the remaining corruption they are often tempted to despair of the power even of grace to effect a real cure.

Peter's Declaration

Yet in Peter's defense of Gentile freedom (Acts 15:8-9) he said that their hearts were purified "by faith." How does faith bring about this marvelous deeper change, and how can we exercise such faith?

In attempting an answer to this question I wish to begin by a simple illustration. Suppose some evening about dusk I say to my wife, "I just turned on the light," and she has the nerve to answer, "No you didn't!" I bravely persist: "But the light came on, didn't it?" She replies: "Yes, but you didn't turn it on." So I back up and try again: "Then the switch on the wall turned it on." But she comes right back: "No it didn't." Now who is right in this little debate?

We both are. She is more fundamentally right because the light bulb is really activated by the surge of electricity which reaches it. My finger has no power. The switch on the wall, in itself, has no power. We have all heard of the African chief who was so impressed by this amazing magic when he first witnessed it in a modern city that he managed to get a light bulb and a wall switch box, and when he got back home he hung the bulb in his little mud hut and nailed the switch box to a post, then invited his people to see the white man's wonder. When they were crowding around, with a flourish he flipped the switch, but obviously nothing happened. He didn't understand that behind the bulb and the switch was an electric supply system.

Faith Alone Is Impotent

So actually we are not sanctified by faith at all. Faith, in itself, has psychological value, and may impart some sense of security, but it is powerless to cleanse our nature. Our sanctification is willed by the Father, it is brought about through the instrumentality of the Word, it is made possible by the blood of Christ, but it is actually accomplished by the personal and supernatural ministry of the Holy Spirit. Heart purity is ascribed to the cross and to the Word as the mediating instruments; the immediate agent is the Holy Spirit.

This Paul makes clear in Romans 8:2. After diagnosing the human problem as indwelling sin, or what he also calls the "law of sin" (Rom. 7:23), and exulting that our deliverance is "through Jesus Christ our Lord" (v. 25), he pinpoints the actual work of grace by announcing: "The law of the Spirit of life has set me free from the law of sin and death" (NIV). If the law of sin and death is still within we are not free from it. If we are free from it, we are free *from* it, not *with* it, just as a child free from the whooping cough no longer has it. But the Holy Spirit is the purifying Agent.[1]

An ascription of the work of sanctification directly to the Holy Spirit is also given in 2 Thessalonians 2:13: "God has chosen you from the beginning for salvation through sanctification by the Spirit and faith in the truth." Faith in the truth opens the soul to the Spirit's sanctifying ministry, but the actual work of sanctification is the prerogative of the Spirit.[2] According to Peter's First Epistle also the validation of God's choice of us is "the sanctifying work of the Spirit" (1:2).

It is apparent therefore that faith does nothing but make connections. It releases power. Yet in that little imaginary debate with my wife I am right also. This is made clear by the words of Jesus to the blind beggar: "What do you want me to do for you?" He thus acknowledges that the miracle will be His work. Yet He proceeds to say: "Receive your sight; your faith has healed you" (Luke 18:40-42). His faith in Jesus, as being able to do it, and his persistence in calling for help, were real causative factors; *for without them the miracle would not have taken place.* So I am vindicated after all: "I just turned the light on." It is correct therefore to say that we are sanctified by faith. Faith is the catalyst.

Faith and Cornelius

How does this relate to Acts 15:8-9? Peter says that the hearts of Cornelius and his friends were purified by faith. In what sense? The primary sense becomes clear when we remember the issue before them. The alternative was the works of the Law. The Judaizers were insisting that the Gentile converts become circumcised and adapt themselves to the law of Moses. To be sanctified by faith was to be sanctified without erecting a system of works but simply by trusting in the WORK God in Christ had already accomplished. Wesley's comment is to the point, and quite adequate: *"by faith*—without concerning themselves with the Mosaic law."[3]

In the interest of absolute clarity, let us return to my little analogy of turning on the light. Suppose I had either been ignorant of the vast supply system already in place or completely distrusted it, and felt it necessary to go out and build my own, at the cost of millions of dollars and much labor and time, then finally having finished it, would come back to the house and flip the switch. That would have been illumination by "works," with a vengeance. Yet in a sense that is what the Judaizers were expecting of the Gentile converts: redo all the preliminary work as if it all depended on them. *Works* is putting your own delivery system in place; *faith* is believing in the adequacy of the system already put in place by God Himself, and simply plugging into it.

The picture is simple, therefore. When Peter preached in the house of Cornelius he was explaining that God in Christ had put into place a complete and adequate delivery system. And even while he was preaching, they simply put their trust in it.

What About the Apostles?

But this is the way it was for Cornelius and his circle. What about the apostles and the others filled with the Spirit on the Day of Pentecost? If God put no difference between the two groups, and baptized one group with the Spirit exactly as He did the other, then Peter and his fellow participants in the original Pentecost must also have been purified by faith. How did faith "work" with them?

First, we need to consider the fact that before Pentecost the "delivery system" for the fulfillment collectively and individually of Joel 2:28-32 and similar promises was not yet in place, so they could not just plug into it. They didn't know where the switch was or what it would do. Therefore it is apparent that the faith which they exercised and which brought them to the purifying experience in the Spirit could only have been the faith of *obedience* and the faith of *expectancy*.

Their confusion, evident in their question, "Lord, is it at this time You are restoring the kingdom to Israel?" shows how completely they missed any true conception of what the promise of the Father or the coming baptism with the Spirit was about. They were still thinking in worldly and political terms. But they were sure of just one thing: Jesus promised that something he called being "baptized with the Holy Spirit" would occur "not many days" off (Acts 1:5), and had commanded them to tarry in Jerusalem for it. They believed Jesus enough to obey His command. For the record tells us that after Christ's Ascension they returned to Jerusalem, entered "the upper room," and that "all with one mind were continually devoting themselves to prayer."

A ten-day prayer meeting can seem like a long time. Were they tempted to abandon their commitment and go back to their fishing, tax booth or other occupations? Did they begin to think that perhaps there had been some kind of a mistake? If they discussed the matter they would each time conclude: "No, we cannot give up. Jesus said we would be baptized with the Holy Spirit, and told us to wait. We haven't the foggiest notion of what being baptized with the Spirit means, or what to expect, or whether or not we will even know when it happens. But we believe Jesus. In fact, we believe Him enough to just stay with it." So they stayed with it.

Harold Ockenga, in his incisive little book, *Power Through Pentecost*, imagines that such a protracted prayer meeting would very likely have discovered them to themselves and humbled them before each other. Peter, especially—Ockenga suggests—got nowhere in prayer until he faced up to some issues, one by one—his fishing nets, his beautiful home overlooking the blue Galilee, the need for providing for his mother-in-law. Each item was surrendered to God; then the Lord would search out something else, including his bad attitude and his ambition to be first.

Notice how graphically Ockenga imagines the struggle: "The question arose in his mind of his willingness to give up his home and travel to far-off heathen countries; to live his life among barbarians, or Greeks, or Romans; to spend the rest of his life in evangelism. Finally, he prayed through that, consecrated his home, agreed to take his wife with him, and, whether in poverty or abundance, to labour with an eye single to the glory of God."[4]

Ockenga suggests that they had a confession meeting, and asked forgiveness of each other for their jealousies and irritations and self-centeredness. Finally when the Day of Pentecost came they were not only physically in one place but spiritually of one accord. They were ready for God's marvelous outpouring of His Spirit.

Therefore for the disciples and the apostles the faith by which they were sanctified could not have been the faith of appropriation, that simply plugs into a fully functional delivery system. It had to be the faith of obedience and the faith of expectancy, which waited in prayer and heart searching and confession and surrender, until the event came.

How Faith "Works" Today

What about us? How are we sanctified "by faith"? First, of course, we go back to Cornelius and remind ourselves that we too must trust in God's provision for our sanctification and make sure that we do not drift into a works mode, of attempting to sanctify ourselves, by discipline, spiritual formation, increasing our service, or trusting in *time* to do what needs to be done. Sanctification is available to us *now*, and it is no more by works for us than it was for Cornelius.

When we were overseas we lived for some time in a small house on a side street, where the residents had been waiting twelve years for the installation of telephone service. Applications had been made, and when you bought a house the application came with it. During all that time residents acted in the faith of expectancy. Finally, while we lived on that street, the crews erected poles and strung wires, and the day came when our house was wired and a phone installed. Now the delivery system was complete. No longer did we have to live by the faith of expectancy; we just picked up the phone and dialed.

This analogy is by no means watertight, but it bears sufficient validity to be helpful. On the Day of Pentecost the delivery system was complete. Now every believer, Peter said on that memorable day, has free and equal access—"For the promise is for you and your children, and for all who are far off, as many as the Lord our God shall call to himself" (Acts 2:39). Tarrying therefore for eight or ten days is not inherently required, for the Holy Spirit has been given to the church and is available in His sanctifying fullness to every member of the church. There is a sense therefore in which it is proper to speak of the faith that simply "plugs into the system." We call it appropriating faith.

This does not mean, however, that this faith by which we are sanctified has in it no conditions, or that it is quite as simple and easy as flipping a switch on a wall. All Biblical faith which receives any grace from the Lord meets the moral and spiritual conditions essential to that grace, or it is mere pretense. There can be no justifying faith apart from repentance and sincere purpose to serve God. There can be no healing faith without a desire for God's glory. And there can be no sanctifying faith without obeying such passages as Romans 12:1-2, where we are exhorted as believers to make a total presentation of our bodies to the Lord as a living sacrifice, and to stop being conformed to this world in any sense in which we still are, and allow ourselves to be transformed by the complete and decisive renewing of the mind, effected by the Holy Spirit.[5]

While an attempt to consecrate will not bring the blessing if it goes on forever and never culminates in an act of appropriating and trusting faith, it is equally true that an easy believism which bypasses the self-crucifixion of rigorous self-examination and equally thorough consecration will not bring the blessing either. John Wesley taught that if believers were to be sanctified wholly by faith they needed to see the ground of their heart. He writes: "A deep conviction that we are not yet whole; that our hearts are not fully purified; that there is yet in us a 'carnal mind,' which is still in its nature 'enmity against God'; that a whole body of sin remains in our hearts"—this conviction will show, he adds, "the absolute necessity of a farther change."[6] "For," he says, "till we are sensible of our disease, it admits of no cure."[7]

It is for this reason that most Christians need to exercise the faith of obedience and the faith of expectation, just as the disciples did, before they can properly exercise the faith of appropriation. Generally this takes some time. There must be time to allow the Holy Spirit to discover our real need to us, and create in us a hunger deep enough that it will not be short- circuited into chronic shallowness by a premature faith-claim. As D. Willia Caffray used to say, "A heart that is not submitted for searching will not be undertaken for cleansing."

Too many have claimed by faith a "work" of grace that never really "worked." I recall a lady in a southern Idaho town who was at the altar seeking heart holiness every night for 22 days. She prayed louder and longer than any other seeker. Her hands were upraised and so was her voice. At the beginning I said to myself: "It won't take long for this lady to get through, for she is in dead earnest." But she didn't get through. After a few nights I tried to get a few words in edgewise about the importance of faith, but without slowing down she answered me in her prayer by saying, "Lord, You know I took it by faith a year ago and nothing happened. I want something I can know about." That silenced me, because I wanted her to have something she could know about also.

Finally the last night of the revival came. All the other seekers had prayed through and gone home. She was still storming the heavens, supported by a few embattled, weary saints, who also were praying loudly. I was desperate, because I hated to see the meeting close with her not in victory. I believe the Spirit prompted me to command her and everyone else to stop praying. When things had shuddered to a stop I said, "Now I want everyone around this sister to pray one prayer inwardly—not aloud—'Lord, put Your finger on the one thing that is keeping her out of blessing.' " Then I said to the seeker: "You pray the same prayer, inwardly, not a word out loud: "Lord, put Your finger on the one thing keeping me out of blessing.'" For a few moments there was blissful silence, then I heard her begin to whisper, "Yes, Lord!" In a few moments her yes became louder and more decisive, and shortly she was on her feet giving her testimony.

She confessed that during all those weeks God had been trying to speak to her about a particular issue, on which there was between her and the Lord a battle of wills. She had argued that the matter was so small it couldn't possibly be her problem. And to avoid facing it she had tried to drown God's voice out with her loud praying, supposing that if she could just make enough noise she could badger God for the blessing on her own terms. But it was all wasted effort. Incidentally, I saw her three months later and she was still radiant.

The moral: Faith will not work as long as there is the tiniest controversy between us and the Lord. But when we resolve the issue of full obedience it will be quite natural for faith to receive. As Arthur Climenhaga says: "There is no such thing as naked faith. Real faith is clothed. It is clothed with surrender and obedience, and will bring reality."

Breaking the Faith Barrier

While generally it is natural to believe when we have met conditions, there are times when the faith barrier must be broken by a deliberate decision to claim by faith as a present blessing what God has promised, simply because He has promised it, and is totally trustworthy. This was E. Stanley Jones' experience; it was Samuel Brengle's experience; and many others. For there is a certain fear and hesitancy in casting ourselves completely on the promises of God, without any supporting props of feelings or signs or evidences. But we must keep in mind certain axiomatic truths. One is that unbelief is sin, for it is a reflection on the integrity of God. A second truth is that as unbelief was the first sin, so often it is the last to be renounced. A third axiomatic truth is that if we believe only when propped up by evidences, we are believing the evidences, not the Word of God.

It could be that there is a connection here with Jesus' phrasing in John 17:17—"Sanctify them in the truth; Thy word is truth." Alter the phrasing and Jesus is saying, "Sanctify them in the sphere of God's Word." God's Word delineates and assures us of the delivery system I have been talking about, and is therefore what is to be believed (cf. Acts 10:32). God's truth makes provision for our sanctification. If the Spirit is going to be enabled to make this sanctification real to us we must believe and accept as ours the provision about which we read in the Word. Our assurance must be grounded in our absolute faith in the Word, which is to say, the integrity of God.

In many cases God is pleased to give an emotional experience of assurance at the time of believing. That is wonderful, but it does not add to the reality of the event. And down the line, God will withdraw this emotional prop, and we will find it necessary to stand solidly on God's Word, without a bit of feeling. God's will is that we be sanctified, and the promise is: "The one who calls you is faithful, and he will do it" 1 Thess 5:24 (NIV). When? When we ask Him, when we meet conditions, and when we trust Him for the blessing.

ENDNOTES

1. Also in Romans is Paul's testimony that his boldness with them as a church is due to his responsibility to so minister to them as a "priest" that his "offering of the Gentiles might become acceptable, sanctified by the Holy Spirit" (Rom. 15:16; literally, *having been* sanctified by the Holy Spirit). As A. T. Robertson points out, it is the Gentiles who are to be sanctified, not the offering considered as an act in itself (*Word Pictures in the New Testament* [New York: Harper & Brothers, Publishers, 1931), Vol. IV, p. 420). Unless the Gentile converts are personally sanctified by the inward work of the Holy Spirit they are not yet acceptable, because not yet clean. Appropriate is the comment of Wilber Dayton, that the apostle felt it essential that he stay with his Gentile converts until fruit was borne "not only in the forgiveness of sins but in a genuine purification and dedication of life through the Holy Spirit that would make the people a suitable present to God." (*The Wesleyan Biblical Commentary* [Grand Rapids: William B. Eerdmans Publishing Company, 1965], Vol. V, p. 90).

2. It would be tempting to bear down on the implication: No sanctification, no salvation.

3. *Notes on the New Testament*.

4. *Power Through Pentecost* (Grand Rapids: Wm. B. Eerdmans Publishing Company, 1959), p. 33.

5. See Thayer for *anakainōsis*.

6. Sermon "Repentance of Believers," *Works*, Vol. p. 168f.

7. Ibid., p. 165.

8. For a discussion of Phoebe Palmer's formula concerning the altar sanctifying the gift, see Richard S. Taylor, *Exploring Christian Holiness*, Vol. III, "The Theological Formulation," pp. 179-182; see also Ray Dunning, *Grace, Faith, and Holiness*, pp. 467-469.

CHAPTER THREE

Perfecting Holiness: Crisis or Process?

This chapter studies a passage which some of us believe is exegetically and theologically crucial to Wesleyanism. The NASB renders it as follows: "Therefore, having these promises, beloved, let us cleanse ourselves from all defilement of flesh and spirit, perfecting holiness in the fear of God."

This obviously is the climax of the previous exhortation to be separate from the world, and should never have been severed from it by a chapter division. (When Jesus said, "What God hath joined together let not man put asunder," He could very well have added, "Let not chapter dividers separate what belongs together!")

The Nature of the Need

Paul starts the paragraph in 6:14 with the command, "Do not be bound together with unbelievers," and proceeds to argue the incompatibility between what belongs to Christ and what belongs to Satan, between light and darkness, and between the clean and the unclean. The necessity of separation is predicated on our identity as "the temple of the living God" (v. 16). It is because of this that God promises, " 'I will dwell in them and walk among them; and I will be their God, and they shall be my people' " (v. 16b, from Exod. 29:45; Lev. 26:12; Jer. 31:1). Now comes the first "Therefore": " 'Therefore' [*because of this promise*], 'come out from their midst and be separate,' says the Lord. 'And do not touch what is unclean' " (v. 17, from Isa. 52:11). The promise " 'And I will welcome you' " (v. 17c) is contingent upon obeying the command to come out and touch not. Equally contingent is the promise which follows: " 'And I will be a father to you, And you shall be sons and daughters to Me,' says the Lord Almighty" (v. 18). The unknown Scripture Paul is quoting here declares our very relation to God as sons and daughters to depend on this radical severance from the world and its defilement.

Now comes the second "Therefore," the grand conclusion, which is the text before us: "Therefore, having these promises, beloved, let us cleanse ourselves from all defilement of flesh and spirit, perfecting holiness in the fear of God" (7:1).

We are not necessarily to understand from Paul's insistence on separation that these Corinthians were involved in overt worldliness or sins of the flesh. According to Paul's testimony of them in 1 Corinthians 6:9-11, they had been saved out of the gross life-style of their previous paganism. A radical separation and transformation had already taken place. But the fact that Paul also was compelled to dub them as "yet carnal" (KJV), would suggest that he saw in them some worldly tendencies and affinities which could yet be their undoing if not faced up to forthrightly and forestalled by a radical cleansing, at a deeper level than they had yet experienced.

The first half of the verse is straight forward enough and occasions no particular controversy. The aorist tense of *katharisomen*, "let us cleanse," implies more than a polite suggestion; it is rather a challenge to act at once, decisively, and thoroughly in cleansing ourselves from all contamination of our flesh and spirit. Obviously such a cleansing is far more than external severance with practices and associations displeasing to God, but an internal housecleaning as well. To be cleansed in spirit is to be sanctified in heart. It is to be delivered from any affinity in our spirit with the appeal of the world and its evil, so that we are emancipated by a radical alienation from it in our desires and affections.

Obviously, while we are challenged to do this ourselves, we can only do what lies within our power to do. This includes separation, renunciation, confession and total surrender. It also includes laying hold through prayer and faith of the power of the Spirit to internalize the cleansing at a level beyond the reach of our own will. But we are told to so cleanse ourselves because the responsibility for action, including appropriation, is ours.

The Exegetical Issue

The controversy arises in knowing how to relate the first half of the verse, the cleansing from all contamination of flesh and spirit, with the second half, "perfecting holiness in the fear of the Lord." Because the participle *epitelountes*, "perfecting," is in the present tense, some Wesleyans have interpreted the verse to combine within itself both the crisic and progressive aspects of Christian holiness. The aorist *katharisomen*, "let us cleanse," is said to express the punctiliar side of sanctification, while the perfecting is said to express the ongoing striving toward complete holiness.

Some of us believe strongly that such an exegesis is not only incorrect grammatically, but a critical error theologically, for by implication it defines holiness primarily as maturity rather than primarily as purity. The emphasis is thus on process rather than on crisis. This opens a pandora box concerning the doctrine of holiness.[1]

While the origin of this approach is uncertain, it has been credited to Daniel Steele. In *Mile-stone Papers*, published in 1878, he says that "the duty enjoined in II Cor. 7:1, of perfecting holiness, is a progressive work, realizing, or carrying into practice, the cleansing from all filthiness instantaneously wrought within."[2] However, he apparently changed his mind, for in *Half-Hours With St. Paul*, published 16 years later, in 1894, again speaking of this verse, he says that "all filthiness of the flesh and spirit" is to be "cleansed in the act of 'perfecting holiness.' "[3] It is clear therefore that it would be questionable scholarship to cite Steele as an authority for the "gradual" interpretation.

On the other side of the water, the view may have originated with William Burt Pope, who does espouse it in no uncertain terms.[4] Strangely, however, Pope treats the cleansing as gradual and progressive, as well as the perfecting in holiness, ignoring the significance of the aorist tense for cleansing.

As for John Wesley, citations can be found on both sides of the issue. In his *Notes* he comments on the second half of the verse: "Yet let us not rest in negative religion, but *perfect holiness*—carrying it to the height in all its branches."[5] Yet twenty-three years later (1777), in the finally revised edition of his *Plain Account of Christian Perfection,* Wesley relates 2 Corinthians 7:1 to Ezekiel 36:29 as the New Testament fulfillment. He says: "No promise can be more clear. And to this the Apostle plainly refers in that exhortation: 'Having these promises, let us cleanse ourselves from all filthiness of flesh and spirit, perfecting holiness in the fear of God.' " Immediately he supports this with what he calls "that ancient promise: 'The Lord thy God will circumcise thy heart.' "[6] The implication here seems to be that at this point Wesley sees the two halves of the verse in the common sense and customary way of viewing it, viz., that the two clauses exactly interface. That is, the perfecting of the holiness is the simple counterpart of the cleansing.

While Wesley's sermon on "The Circumcision of the Heart" antedates both his *Notes* and his *Plain Account* by many years (preached first in 1733), it contains a reference to 2 Corinthians 7:1 which may reasonably be seen as Wesley's normative view. In defining circumcision of the heart he says: "It is that habitual disposition of soul which, in the sacred writings is termed holiness; and which directly implies, the being cleansed from sin, 'from all filthiness both of flesh and spirit;' and, by consequence, the being endued with those virtues which were also in Christ Jesus; . . ."[7] Here the cleansing of 2 Corinthians 7:1 is identified as the cleansing of circumcision, and is equally identified with holiness, as the term is normatively intended in the Scriptures.

This is the understanding found in Adam Clarke, Richard Watson, and the major Methodistic theologians right down to Wiley, George Turner, William Greathouse, and Wilber T. Dayton—to mention but four in this century.[8]

The More Natural Exegesis

Rather than dismembering this simple verse, and abandoning what is the plain meaning as read in English, it is better to see *epitelountes*, "perfecting," as a temporal participle, the action of which coincides with the action of the main verb, *kathrarisomen*, "let us cleanse." So Ralph Earle says: " 'Let us cleanse' is in the aorist (hortatory) subjunctive, suggesting an instantaneous crisis of cleansing, rather than a process. 'Perfecting' is a present participle, indicating action simultaneous with that of the main verb—'let us cleanse.' The clear sense of the Greek is that 'perfecting holiness' is synonymous, or at least concomitant, with the crisis of cleansing."[9]

Two further exegetical details lend support to this simple, common sense position. First, the addition of *epi* to *teleō* in *epitelountes* adds the force of urgency. This is seen in the way this compound is used by Paul elsewhere. In the very next chapter this word is used three times in respect to the money-raising project for the poor in Jerusalem. In 8:6 it is translated by the word "complete"—"Consequently we urged Titus that as he had previously made a beginning, so he would also complete in you this gracious work." In v. 11 the same word is used twice, translated "finish" and "completion," as follows: "But now finish doing it also; that just as there was the readiness to desire it, so there may be also the completion of it by your ability." While the definiteness obviously intended is not necessarily a moment which can be registered by the clock (as a completion at 10 p.m. Sunday night), it *is* such a definiteness as to rule out any extended length of time. Any idea of gradualism as an acceptable fulfillment is expressly excluded. This has already been too much the problem, and Paul is wanting them not just to "get on with it" but to get it *done*.[10]

This usage of Paul argues for a similar intention in 2 Corinthians 7:1. He does not have in mind a switch from punctilear action to progressive, drawn out action, but uses *epitelountes* with the sense of an immediate obligation to complete thoroughly the holiness which up to now has been partial and unsatisfactory. The obligation to get rid of personal contamination is immediate—right now—and the perfecting of holiness is simply a positive way of expressing what is done when the cleansing is done.

A second exegetical consideration is the word for holiness, *hagiōsyne*. It is found only two other times in the New Testament, both of them in Paul's writings, Romans 1:4, where we have the expression, "the Spirit of holiness" (NIV), and 1 Thessalonians 3:13, where we have the phrase "unblamable in holiness." Thayer defines the word as used in Corinthians and Thessalonians simply as "moral purity." This means that the word is peculiarly appropriate for the subject matter of the exhortation of the passage before us. A cleansing from sin—the opposite of moral purity—has just been urged upon these believers; when that is experienced moral purity will be enjoyed as the consequence.

Clearly therefore, this word will not tolerate gradualism any more than *epitelountes*. God does not authorize a gradual attainment of moral purity. Indeed, to suppose that God through Paul is admonishing these Corinthians to get rid of sin at once, then gradually complete the work of moral purifying, is self-contradictory.

The Theological Issues

Now to make the transition from the exegetical argument to the theological, this proposition is in order: When the believer completes the cleansing from all contamination of flesh and spirit he is then perfectly holy. This is theologically crucial because it limits the concept of holiness to a state of grace available now and delimits it from a state of maturity which is achieved gradually.

As has already been seen the peculiar word used by Paul in this passage argues for this understanding. But other words in the Greek also denote a purity and hallowedness which are immediately obligatory—exactly what the English word "holiness" conveys to the Biblically informed layman. To extend the word holiness to an amoral meaning is confusing, to say the least, and completely without exegetical support elsewhere.[11]

Let us press this further. If all contamination of flesh and spirit is cleansed, any unholiness which remains must of necessity be in the nature of something other than sin. What is it? Ignorance? Infirmity? Immaturity? Amoral faults of personality, such as bad table manners? Such a notion violates every traditional concept of holiness. Holiness is the opposite of unholiness. Unholiness is some degree or form of sin, and sin is always a condition demanding immediate correction. If holiness is a quality or condition beyond purity, then unholiness also is a quality or condition beyond impurity, and must be some form of human limitation not amenable to immediate cleansing.

This is to trifle with the word holiness, and introduce endless confusion into the doctrine. Holiness must never be thought of as an amoral quality. Even the hallowedness of positional holiness, or sanctity based on relationship with Christ, is not amoral, as if it could exist independently of moral purity. There is, indeed, a fine distinction between the two in definition, but not a separation in fact. Positional sanctity is invalidated by a failure to match sanctity with sanctification.

A further theological flaw in the interpretation at issue is the implication that holiness suddenly becomes an *ideal* toward which we strive, *not* a spiritual base on which we *build*. This, of course, is a growth theory of holiness. An acute question which we confront at once is the matter of terminus: when do we reach this perfected holiness? If holiness includes an amoral quality of personality or knowledge or skill, how are we to know when such a deficiency is sufficiently supplied for

1 Corinthians 7:1 to have been fulfilled? Or is the perfecting simply a life-long striving to be as holy as possible? This is good Calvinism, but it is poor Wesleyanism.

In thus confusing holiness with maturity we become guilty of fostering what H. Orton Wiley and others have declared to be the fountainhead of most of the misapprehensions and misrepresentations relating to the Wesleyan doctrine of Christian perfection.[12] The normal viewpoint of the Scriptures is that holiness, without which no one will see the Lord, is a state or condition morally obligatory and personally possible in the present, a condition available through grace and the inward work of the Holy Spirit on clearly defined moral terms. It is a covenant relationship of entire devotement to God, and in its normative and full sense implies the cleansing of the heart from all sin, and the establishment of love as the master motive of life.

Holiness and Growth

Some persons might object to the stringent definition here being advocated by saying that growing in holiness is growing in strength of Christlike character. That there is such growth is certainly to be expected, and is probably what Wesley meant by his expression "Carrying it to the height in all its branches." The branches of holiness may be designated as Christlikeness of personality, sturdiness of faith, power in prayer, stability of character, and such areas of needed growth. But these areas of progress do not represent becoming more holy, in the essential sense of the term.

Supposing we take the position that becoming *stronger* is becoming more holy. In this case holiness is at least partially defined as strength and unholiness would at least partially have to be defined as weakness. If we draw a rectangle and bisect it by a diagonal line from the lower left corner to the upper right corner, we can write HOLINESS in one triangle and WEAKNESS in the other, with the diagonal line representing

GROWTH. As the growth moves up the diagonal line, it becomes apparent that holiness increases and weakness decreases. (Fig. 1)

Now, if we shift to the core issue before us, we can cross

Figure 1

out the word WEAKNESS and in its place put the word SIN. This model says that the opposite of holiness is sin. (Fig. 2) As we move up the line of growth sin decreases and holiness increases. But since we may die before we get very far, we must cut the line off somewhere toward the right hand corner by death. In this case we will never complete the perfecting of holiness short of dying.

The correct model is to see the entire rectangle as holi-

Figure 2

ness. We are made holy by regeneration and sanctification. Within this holiness rectangle is the diagonal line of growth, but on either side, i.e., above and below, are neither weakness nor sin as the antithesis of holiness; rather we see immaturity/ignorance as the antithesis of maturity, so that as we progress up the growth line there is not a progressive increase in holiness but a progressive increase in maturity and decrease in immaturity. (Fig. 3)

On this model there is growth within holiness, not into it. Holiness needs to be maintained by obedience, deep devotion, continued trust, in short, by walking "in the light." But a

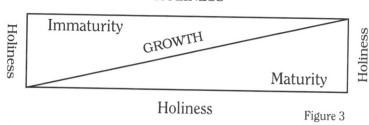

HOLINESS

Figure 3

mature saint is not essentially more holy than he was when regenerated and entirely sanctified. He is however stronger in holiness, more adult in his understanding of its implications, more skilled in its expression, and doubtless more exemplary in its representation. For holiness is a state both of moral purity and entire devotement to God, a state we may enter now, and without which the growth will be stalemated.

May I summarize: Let us steadfastly maintain the traditional distinction between holiness and maturity. The antithesis of holiness is sin, while the antithesis of maturity is weakness and ignorance. Growth in grace is relevant to maturity; it is not relevant to holiness. While we sometimes speak of becoming "established in holiness" this is not equivalent to an increase in holiness. As J. B. Chapman once wrote: "There is no state of grace beyond a pure heart filled with the Holy Spirit. . . . Holiness is purity—not maturity."[13]

Perhaps someone objects, "But does not the expression 'perfecting holiness' imply the possibility of an imperfect holiness?" Yes, truly so, but the imperfect holiness precedes this radical cleansing, it does not follow it. Its imperfection is to be brought to an end. Imperfect holiness is the great peril; therefore we are admonished to perfect it in "the fear of the Lord." And if our "fear of the Lord" is deep enough we will do it now.

ENDNOTES

1. That Calvinistically inclined translators would lean this way is understandable. When the trial edition of the NIV New Testament came out this phrase was rendered, "and let us strive for perfection"—leaving out "holiness" altogether. This was such an obvious mangling that a position paper was sent to the committee by Wesleyan scholars urging a revision. (Other passages were of concern also.) Fortunately, with the weight of Ralph Earle on board, they heeded our request, with the result that when the entire Bible was published the verse read: "Since we have these promises, dear friends, let us purify ourselves from everything that contaminates body and spirit, perfecting holiness out of reverence for God."

I note, however, that *The New Translation: The Letters of the New Testament,* put out this year (1990) by The Society for *The New Translation,* and distributed by Tyndale House, translates as follows: "And so, dear friends, since we have these promises, let us cleanse ourselves from everything that pollutes *us in* either body or spirit, striving for holiness in the fear of God." Getting "striving" out of *epitelountes* is an amazing bit of verbal acrobatics.

2. Minneapolis, MN: Bethany Fellowship, reprint, nd., p 107.

3. Boston: The Christian Witness Co., 1894, p. 91.

4. *A Compendium of Christian Theology* (London: Wesleyan Conference Office, 1880), pp. 39-41.

5. *Explanatory Notes on the New Testament* (New York: Phillips & Hunt, n.d.; originally published 1754).

6. *Works,* Vol. XI, p. 389. It is odd that, whereas Sangster cites 2 Corinthians 7:1 as one of Wesley's 30 proof texts, there is no sermon on it in his *Works.*

7. *Works,* Vol. V, p. 203.

8. Apparently Ray Dunning also sees no special problem here, for he cites this verse as one of Wesley's proof texts that

we can expect to be saved from all sin in this life. *Grace, Faith, and Holiness* (Kansas City, MO: Beacon Hill Press of Kansas City, 1988), p. 463. Dunning has no other reference to this passage in his volume.

9. Personal note to this writer. See also George Turner, *The Vision Which Transforms* (Kansas City, MO: Beacon Hill Press of Kansas City), p. 123.

10. See also Romans 15:28; Galatians 3:3; Phil. 1:6. On the last Ralph Earle says: "The best rendering here is 'bring it to completion,' " and he cites RSV, NEB, Berk. (*Word Meanings in the New Testament* (Kansas City, MO: Beacon Hill Press of Kansas City, 1977], Vol. 5, p. 14).

11. Because *hagiasmos* is an action noun, some have sought to make a case for the view that it always refers to the process of being sanctified. That there is a processive aspect of sanctification, in the broad sense of the term, may be conceded. What cannot be conceded is that any degree of unholiness in the sense of sinfulness is temporarily tolerable, or to be seen as a problem to be corrected gradually. The definiteness of the word with the article, "the sanctification without which no one will see the Lord" (Heb. 12:14, NASB) argues for a recognizable and knowable condition rather than a vague, unmeasurable process. Procksch's denotation of *hasiasmos* in this verse as "a moral goal" (Kittel, 1:113) is hardly compatible with its necessity for seeing the Lord. If we are to see the Lord *hagiasmos* must be an experiential reality currently; otherwise the Christian life would exist under a shadow of uncertainty. An immediate need cannot be satisfied by an aim toward an unreached goal. *Hagiasmos* as an action noun means primarily that it is a work of divine grace wrought in the believer and not a generic or self-achieved state. The weight of emphasis is not on the action but on the result of the action. See Arndt and Gingrich.

12. H. Orton Wiley, *Christian Theology* (Kansas City, MO: Nazarene Publishing House, 1941), vol. 2, p. 506.

13. *Holiness, the Heart of Christian Experience* (Kansas City, MO: Nazarene Publishing House, 1943), p. 10.

CHAPTER FOUR

Temptation and Sin: Are Temptable Desires Sinful?

My thesis in this chapter is that the translation of *epithumia* by "lust," as in NASB, KJV, NEB, et al., in James 1:13-15, has very grave implications for the understanding of the nature of temptation, and extensive negative corollaries touching the doctrines of sin, man, and grace. A hint of the issues can be stated this way: If temptation implies that the desires to which they appeal are already sinful, then we are hard put to account for the temptation of Adam and Eve in the garden, and even more baffled in accounting for the temptation of Jesus in the wilderness.[1]

Lust or Desire?

We can avoid impalement on the horns of this dilemma if we follow RSV, Amplified, Moffatt, Goodspeed, and Phillips in translating *epithumia* by "desire." Strong desire is the simple basic meaning of the word. In itself the word is morally neutral. Jesus used it when He said to His disciples, *"epithumia epethumesa*—with great desire I have desired to eat this Passover with you" (Luke 22:15; cf Phil.1:23).

The issue is crucial in the James passage for two reasons. First, the kind of *peirasmos*, "temptation," which is the focus of James' attention in vv. 13-15 is obviously not the more usual "trial" or "test" but an enticement to sin. When therefore we translate *epithumia* by "lust" we are implying an interpretation, viz., that the passage teaches the prior sinfulness of temptable desires. In contrast the simple translation of *epithumia* by "desire" leaves the door open for a different understanding of temptation.

The second reason this passage is crucial is the fact that the proposition is stated as a universal: "Each one," as NASB puts it, "is tempted when he is drawn away and enticed by his own lust." This means that all temptation presupposes the presence of lust, or evil desire. This implies that if there is no prior evil desire there can be no temptation. Hence, persons without sinful desires are untemptable, including Adam and Eve and Jesus.

The untemptability of God is firmly declared: "For God cannot be tempted by evil" (v. 15). But God's untemptability is not due to his purity of desire alone, but to an absolute, sovereign holiness which is impervious to the seductive approach of Satan, and totally free from suggestions toward evil arising from within himself. Furthermore, God is not a moral creature on trial, as is man. Even the Second Adam subjected Himself to the recapitulation of the test of the First Adam; which implies that temptability was endemic to the Incarnation (cf. Heb. 2:14-18). It also implies that strong desire does not need to be sinful to be the object of temptation.

Desire and Enticement

We will return to our analysis of Christ's temptation later. But in the meanwhile let us look again at James and see exactly what he says. It is debatable whether the phrase *hupo tēs idias epithumias* "by his own desire," governs both *exelkomenos* "drawn out," and *deleazomenos*, "enticed," or only the first. The majority opinion seems to be that the desire or craving is responsible for both movements, the drawing out and the enticement: so TCNT, "A man is in every case tempted by his own passions— allured and enticed by them."[2]

However some strong voices can be found favoring the view that the enticement is distinct from and external to the movement of the desire. KJV implies this in its punctuation (though the NKJV removes the comma). Williams says "and enticed by a bait."[3] So also A. T. Robertson: "Allured by definite bait."[4] This is supported by the word itself, *deleazō*, "to bait, catch by a bait," with an extended meaning, "to beguile by blandishments, allure, entice, deceive" (Thayer).[5] This is the work of an outside influence, playing on the desire. Fish do not set their own bait, but move out to take the bait placed by the fisherman.

Thayer, Robertson, and Arndt & Gingrich all call attention to Philo's relevant expression, "enticed by pleasure."[6] This phrase recognizes two fundamental elements in the psychology of temptation. One is that sin is tempting only when it promises pleasure. The very nature of temptation is to hide the pain which is sin's ultimate consequence. The hook is covered by the bait. If no pleasure or satisfaction were promised, the offer would hold no appeal. This is true with both holy and unholy desire. The difference is that the pleasure grasped by holy desire is in itself holy and is enduring, while the pleasures of sin are tarnished, debasing, and fleeting. But temptation in its very nature involves the obscuring of this fact.

The second fundamental element suggested by Philo's phrase in the nature of temptation is the presentation to the eyes or to the mind the pleasure as something available. Temptation constitutes an offer. It is a beckoning situation. The desires are stimulated and drawn out by what one perceives to be an immediate or at least a reachable possibility. The suggestion that I fly to the moon under my own power could hardly be called a temptation.

The Source of Temptation

If the phenomenon of temptation cannot be explained on the basis of desire alone, but must involve external influence, what could such influence be? James opens the paragraph by declaring that temptation cannot be ascribed to God. "Let no one say when he is tempted, I am being tempted by God. God cannot be tempted with evil, and he himself does not tempt anyone" (v. 13). On this verse A. T. Robertson comments: "It is contemptible, but I have heard wicked and weak men blame God for their sins."[7]

W. E. Oesterley suggests that James here might be rebuking the notion held by many Jewish rabbis that God was indirectly responsible for at least temptation's inordinate power for having created man with the *Yetser-hara'*, the tendency to evil which exists in man together with the *Yetser ha-tob'*, the tendency to good. In discussing a possible connection here Oesterley says that after many theories and long debate the rabbis drifted to the conclusion "that God, as the Creator of all things, must have also created the *Yetser hara'*."[8] To believe this would provide people with a convenient cop-out for their sins. But James closes this escape hatch by the flat declaration that God can neither be tempted nor is it morally possible for Him to tempt anyone else to do wrong. This carries with it the implication that God could not have created a nature in man which would constitute a predisposition toward responding to temptation. Man's nature in that case would have been bent toward evil prior to trial, which would have placed him from the moment of creation at an unfair disadvantage. The Creator who thus created could not have escaped sharing moral responsibility for the consequences.

The doctrine of primitive holiness postulates the exact opposite situation: that the holy God created a holy being, with a predisposition to love and obey, and placed him in an ideal environment, so that the advantage was on his side, thus making man solely responsible for his moral response, and taking from him forever any basis for blaming God. Adam did blame God,[9] but that was a manifestation of his now fallen nature; it was not a rational or justifiable complaint. The sum of the matter is that God is neither directly nor indirectly the source of temptation.

The Biblical answer to the question of external sources is expressed by Carl G. Kromminga, "Enticement to sin and to impatient rebellion is the work of Satan," and he refers to Rev. 2:9; 1 Pet. 5:8-9; cf. 1 Thess. 3:5.[10] William Watson is even more to the point. He says: "St. James describes the course which

temptation when unresisted takes. . . . In the sense of enticement to evil it is Satan that tempts men. He is the tempter."[11]
Obviously this position finds its prime examples in the two
classic cases of temptation in Biblical history, that in the garden and that in the wilderness, in both of which Satan was the
seducer.

In the ordinary day-by-day temptations which most of us
experience the hand of Satan is hidden. Nevertheless he is the
tempter, though he utilizes demons and evil people. Demons
have access to our minds with their suggestions and rational-
izations, while evil people are Satan's accomplices by their
example, persuasion, and their diabolical ability to make evil
available and to make it attractive.

The Garden and Wilderness Temptations

Avoiding the loaded term "lust" in James' universal
proposition leaves us free to see that while some temptable
desires are sinful, not all are. If holy desires are temptable then
the problem of accounting for Adam and Eve's vulnerability
and explaining how the sinless Son of God could be tempted
disappears.

What were the desires appealed to in the garden? "When
the woman saw that the tree was good for food, that it was a
delight to the eyes, and that the tree was desirable to make one
wise, she took from its fruit and ate" (Gen. 3:6). Camouflaging
the real issues, Satan via the serpent appealed to the desires
for food, for beauty, and for wisdom. Satan promised appetitive
satisfaction, aesthetic pleasure, and intellectual understanding. What could be more innocent and natural than these
desires? What was there therefore in Satan's reasoning which
made his approach a temptation to sin? It was not in the suggestion that these desires be satisfied, but that they be satisfied
in the wrong way—by disobedience to God.

This pattern is repeated with remarkable similarity in the
wilderness. Here too Satan offered satisfaction for three very

legitimate, sinless desires. Jesus was hungry. The first temptation was directed at this desire: "command that these stones be made bread" (Matt. 4:3). Jesus desired, very properly, without any taint of sin, to be accepted as the Messiah by His own people. The second temptation played on that desire. The third desire, to rule the world, was equally proper, indeed a desire destined for ultimate fulfillment. But in each attack the element in Satan's suggestion which constituted it a temptation was the *modus operandi* of fulfillment: to grasp for immediate fulfillment at the expense of God's will and God's program. Have not the most devout saints of the centuries felt the force of this kind of temptation assaulting them at the point of their holiest desires?

And there was an ascending scale of gravity: first, that Jesus prove His divinity by satisfying His hunger; second, that He prove His Messiahship by the spectacular demonstration of the supernatural; third—Satan's real objective—that He achieve world rule by transferring allegiance. In this temptation Satan revealed his hand. All subtleties were cast aside. It was a raw, desperate bid to rule as God. This is the underlying goal in all temptation. Here is the epitome of the cosmic struggle— Satan's age-long lust for the throne of God would be fulfilled if he could but abort the mission of the God-Man by tricking Him into the tiniest deviation from the Father's plan and the Father's claims.

Satan's cunning is disclosed. The Divine Throne was beyond his reach, but the moment the Second Person of the Trinity became man Satan had a divine-human target, for the Incarnation brought Jesus into his domain, a domain claimed from God in the garden.[12] Our Lord's temptability as true man became Satan's final chance to unseat the Father. In that attempt Satan was defeated, but his efforts are now focused on Christ's people for every successful temptation is in some sense a demonstration of his lingering hold on the human race, and therefore an embarrassment to God. Temptation, as far as

Satan is concerned, always has as its objective not just the defeat of a person, but the defeat and dishonor of God. Therefore the Christian should be aware that when caught in the throes of temptation he is an actor in the cosmic struggle between good and evil, God and Satan.

When we read that Jesus was tempted in all points like as we are (Heb. 4:15) we are to understand by "points" not the detailed experiences of the 20th century, but the basic categories of human moral conflict—physical, soulish, and spiritual. Temptation involves *ourselves*: *our* appetites and needs. It involves our *relation to others*, including our desire to be liked and accepted. Hundreds of temptations fall into this category. It involves, even more fundamentally, our *relation to God*: our ultimate values and allegiance. Will it be heaven or mammon? God or self?

Some Corollaries

I have sought to make a case for the thesis that temptation does not imply or require the presence of sinful desires, but that rather holy desires are susceptible to temptation. It is time now to show the bearing which this view of temptation has on the doctrines of sin, man, and grace.

In respect to the *doctrine of sin* we need to accept at full face value James' assertion that temptation when yielded to results in sin. This means that sin is a possible outcome and therefore must not be confused with the temptation itself. The statement, "Temptation is not sin" is almost an aphorism among evangelicals. But are we willing to hold to this consistently? If so we will insist that *hamartia* is not the inevitable child of *epithumia* since between the *epithumia* and the sin is the temptation, which is a match-maker's attempt to bring the will into union with the desire. The attempt may be resisted by the will and thus the temptation thwarted.

James says, "Then when desire has conceived it brings forth sin." There is no sin until desire conceives. Conception requires two parents, not one. Implicit here is the assumption of a personal moral agent making a conscious moral decision. As long as the will unwaveringly resists the temptation there is no sin. And the desire which by its very nature is drawn out by the enticement is not proven to be sinful by the fact that the person's desire may be sufficiently strong that he feels a powerful tug, involving a struggle. It is conceivable that in some cases the nature of the temptation may be such that the struggle continues through a period of time without sin being committed, due to the steadfast resistance of the person's determined stand.

The relation of temptation to the *doctrine of man* is equally crucial. Man's temptability is a testimony of and a tribute to his dignity as a transcendent moral being, with links to God unknown to animals. The idea of temptation implies conscious conflict between desire and law. This is a conflict which animals are incapable of experiencing on a self-conscious, rational level. An animal in heat follows blindly yet unerringly its instincts. It experiences no soliloquy respecting proprieties, social obligations, or divine law. But man is a being who can reason: hence capable of thinking ethically. He is moral in the sense that he cannot escape within himself the awareness of right and wrong and a confrontation with these issues. He is religious in his universal propensity to think in terms of approval or disapproval of divine power or powers.

Furthermore, the idea of temptation implies true moral freedom. If this being, even though fallen, is locked into a no-win situation, and has available to him no power to resist temptation, then promise of dignity is aborted and his state becomes one of indignity and slavery. If there is no responsible will arbitrating between the desire and the action we have pure moral determinism. In this case all talk about accountability and responsibility becomes meaningless jargon.

The Possibilities of Grace

But if capability of being tempted is man's glory, his ability to resist temptation is the *glory* of *grace*. The truth of the above paragraph is predicated on grace. Apart from grace man is trapped in the weakness of his own nature, and Skinner indeed has the last word. The freedom of Adam and Eve to choose uncoerced either by outside forces or inside corruption was reduced fatally, so that the natural man is free to sin but not free not to sin—as is so poignantly portrayed in Romans 7. This creates a tragic contradiction between what man essentially is as created and what man actually is through the Fall. The resolution of this impasse is the gift of God as a gift of grace. As John Wesley insisted, no man is actually born exclusively in a state of sinfulness but also under grace, a "prevenient grace" which is one of the unconditional benefits of the Atonement, a kind of grace which while not infusing salvation or relieving one of the obligation of personal decision, nevertheless imparts a sufficient degree of moral ability to make the exercise of moral agency again possible.[13] This possibility functions both at the level of daily temptations and at the fundamental level of electing to acknowledge our election in Christ.

The New Testament promises the sufficiency of God's grace to resist temptation. Paul writes: "No temptation has overtaken you but such as is common to man, and God is faithful, who will not allow you to be tempted beyond what you are able, but with the temptation will provide the way of escape also, that you may be able to endure it" (1 Cor. 10:13).[14] This can only be a promise of grace-imparted ability to endure temptation without sinning.

But a crucial question yet remains. Can we who came into this world sinful be set free from sinful desires, and bear before God holy desires? Adam and Eve were created with holy desires, Jesus possessed only holy desires. Can we be cleansed of unholy desires and become controlled by holy desires? The answer to this question also belongs to the role of divine grace.

Admittedly original sin constitutes a subvolitional push toward a state in which all desires are tainted with selfishness. "But sin," writes the apostle Paul (and he means *the* sin, *hē hamartia*, the inborn sin principle) "taking opportunity through the commandment produced in me coveting of every kind" (Rom. 7:8). Covetous desires are sinful desires. Yet to the Ephesian elders Paul could testify, "I have coveted no man's silver, or gold, or apparel" (Acts 20:33). Somewhere Paul's desires had been purified of covetousness. This possibility is the true glory of grace and of the God of all grace. The possibility of a pure heart implies a renovation of one's desires. We can become mastered by the magnificent obsession of desiring the honor and will of God supremely, with such singlemindedness that all other desires are disciplined by this one dominant passion.

A final possible tangle may need resolution. Perhaps in our thinking we have not always known how to distinguish between holy and unholy desires, and have consequently borne needless guilt. If there is no sin committed until the will endorses and yields to the desire, then the will also governs the moral quality of the desire itself. A desire is not sinful simply because it may be a drawing toward a forbidden object, but only if the desire for this object is inwardly accepted. Only then does it become lust or covetousness. The will is thus *already acting* at that stage of the moral scenario.

This is that kind of sin Jesus referred to in His statement: "Everyone who looks on a woman to lust for her has committed adultery with her already in his heart" (Matt. 5:28). This is not the spontaneous look of admiration; neither is it a spontaneous surge of the libido steadfastly resisted; it is rather a look of choice, which means "I would if I could."

When Paul cited the depravities of the Israelites in the wilderness he exhorted: "Now these things happened as examples for us, that we should not crave evil things, as they also craved" (1 Cor. 10:6). If we *should* not then by the grace of God we *need* not. The fact that at times we may be aware of biological urges and spiritual sensitivities which make temptation possible is not to be confused with craving "evil things." Paul is discussing a moral movement of the mind which is volitional.

Holy desires, on the other hand, include the innocent, morally neutral desires which belong to our human nature, provided they are consecrated to God and disciplined by divine law. My desire for food is not sinful simply because my mouth may water at the sight of another person's apple pie. Neither is my desire for success or pleasure or acceptance sinful in and of itself. But such primitively innocent desires can be kept from sin only by being kept "on the altar." Through the fullness of the Spirit—who is the Great Enabler—and through the supreme love for God He generates within, preoccupying us with spiritual quests and values, even our natural temptable desires can be kept from becoming sinful desires.

Let us then magnify the grace of God in our theology, and equally in our lives. Let us not hobble ourselves with a pessimistic view of temptation, of sin, or of grace; and let us rejoice that temptation is not an evidence of sinfulness at the moment, but an occasion for demonstrating God's power to cleanse us and keep us. Let us watch and pray lest we enter needlessly into temptation (Matt. 26:41); but when God allows it to come may our love for Him break the tempter's power. Then we will emerge stronger, and we will have defeated the enemy and brought glory to our Saviour.

ENDNOTES

1. While a case may be made for the proposition that the English word "lust" is itself neutral, its popular connotation is loaded with negative implications. According to *Webster's Ninth New Collegiate Dictionary* the word usually means an "intense or unbridled sexual desire." "Lasciviousness" is listed as its synonym. It is this usual connotation which creates the issue discussed in this chapter.

2. *The Twentieth Century New Testament*, Moody Bible Institute.

3. Charles B. Williams, *The New Testament: A Translation in the Language of the People*. Moody Bible Institute, 1937 and 1965.

4. A. T. Robertson, *Word Pictures in the New Testament*, Vol. VI, p. 18. Harper & Brothers, 1933.

5. Joseph Henry Thayer, *Greek-English Lexicon of the New Testament*. Zondervan, 1963.

6. William F. Arndt and F. Wilbur Gingrich, *A Greek-English Lexicon of the New Testament and Other Early Christian Literature*. Zondervan (for University of Chicago Press), 1957.

7. Robertson, ibid., p. 17.

8. W. E. Oesterley, "The General Epistle of James," *The Expositor's Greek Testament*, Vol. IV, p. 411.

9. An innuendo of Adam's lame defense, "The woman whom Thou gavest to be with me" (Gen. 3:12).

10, Carl G. Kromminga, "Temptation," *Baker's Dictionary Of Theology*, p. 515.

11. William Watson, "Temptation, Trial," *Dictionary of the Apostolic Church*, Vol. 2, p. 558.

12. Through Adam's default. Cf. John 12:31; 2 Cor. 4:4; Heb. 2:14; 1 John 5:19.

13. His statement is: "For allowing that all the souls of men are dead in sin by *nature*, this excuses none, seeing there is no man that is in a state of mere nature; there is no man, unless he has quenched the Spirit, that is wholly void of the grace of God" (*Works*, Vol. VI, p. 512).

14. On this passage Wesley observes that God's justice "could not punish us for not resisting any temptation if it were so disproportioned to our strength that it was impossible for us to resist it [by divine grace]" (*Works*, ibid., 480). Yet we are to blame if we do not avail ourselves of our resources in Christ, which Paul calls the "whole armor of God" (Eph. 6:10-18).

CHAPTER FIVE

Holy and Human:

What Is Sanctified Human Nature Like?

In various ways the previous chapters have stressed the cornerstone axiom that purity and maturity are distinct, and that every attempt should be made to avoid confusing them. A pure person in the Biblical sense is an entirely sanctified person. But he may nevertheless be very immature.

In this chapter we will first endeavor to pinpoint, in a practical way, the nature of carnality. Then, in contrast, we will seek to define heart purity. Next we will move into a broad examination of maturity. In this examination we will point out the nature and limitations of maturity, and some special problems of the pure but immature. Following this we will try to pull everything together by delineating the parameters of sanctified humanity, and close by a discussion of holiness and the self.

The Nature of Carnality

Supported by the dictionary, most people think of a carnal person as one given over to sensual pleasures and appetites. This is not the sense of the term carnality when used theologically. It is essentially a mind-set toward self and this world. As such it is either incipient or overt enmity against God (Rom. 8:5-8). A modified form of the concept is found in 1 Corinthians 3, where Corinthian Christians are said to be *sarkikos*, "fleshly" (v. 3; *sarkinos*, "fleshy," in v. 1), which seems to mean that the *psyche*, "soul," of the natural man still dominates them too much, keeping them from being truly spiritual and arresting their spiritual development. Their condition is described as "carnal" by the KJV, "worldly" by the NIV, and just plain "fleshly" by the NASB. Among these Christians the manifestation of this condition is not in gross immorality but in unchristlikeness of spirit, in their relationship with each other. Their value system is still shaped too much by what is important to the world—position, prestige, honor, power; and therefore they jockey among themselves for advantage. Their party-spirit, divisiveness, jealousy, and inordinate pride in their gifts, all stem from this inner remaining worldliness of mind-set. The primary enmity against God has been overpowered by a new love for God, but the remaining disposition toward self-sovereignty and worldly values still disturbs their inner life and compromises their outer life. This is the form of carnality which trips up the Christian not yet fully sanctified.

Carnality is a very real dispositional quality of the soul. While it is both counteracted and modified by the grace of regeneration, it can only be eradicated by the baptism with the Holy Spirit. Theologically we are correct in linking this carnal condition with original sin, and the deeper cleansing of heart holiness as cleansing from original sin.

However, in teaching and preaching this there are two very grave perils. One is to permit a conception of carnality which literalizes the circumcision and similar metaphors into a quasiphysical thing. It needs to be carefully explained that expressions such as "body of sin," "root of bitterness," and "flesh" are all metaphors of a spiritual sickness. While Paul virtually personifies the carnal mind in Romans 7, he should not be understood to be implying an independent entity, but an inherited tendency in the self-life.

When this condition is said to be in the heart the meaning is that the locale of the problem is the inner secret spring of life comprising mind, conscience, will, and affections—everything which shapes and directs what a person is and does. This inner spring is poisoned by excessive self-interest, and as a result directs into selfish ends one's goals and values. The Holy

Spirit wants to deal with this condition, and realign the self into a complete conformity to the Cross. This realignment constitutes the purification. The eradication is in the elimination of the condition, not the removal of a thing, or even the removal of a substantive part of one, as in the case of circumcision.

It is difficult to preach Biblical terms so as to be meaningful to the modern psychologically-oriented mind. Every effort must be made to probe mental processes, and find graphic concrete examples. Jealousy, envy, resentment, covetousness, worldlimindedness, malice, self-willfulness, hardness of heart, are all very concrete experiences, which clog the channels of the soul and overcloud the spirit with a heaviness and a sense of condemnation. The Spirit wants to deliver completely from these negative, unchristlike motions in the soul. He does it by getting at the taproot of an unsurrendered ego. When the self allows the house of cards it has built to collapse it stands naked and broken and ready for the Spirit to take over. This is the moment of entire sanctification.

The other peril against which we must be on guard is a failure to distinguish doctrinally and practically between the core of original sin which is eradicable and its lingering effects which are not, but which will cling to us as a life-long plague. William Burt Pope is helpful here. He says that the term Original Sin has two meanings: "it is the individual portion of the common heritage, and it is the common sin that infects the race of man." He designates what is amenable to the cleansing of grace, as follows: "The original sin in its quality as the *sin that dwelleth in* the Me of the soul, as the principle in man that has actual affinity with transgression, as the source and *law of sin which is in my members,* as the animating soul of *the body of this death,* and, finally, as *the flesh with the affections and lusts,* is abolished by the SPIRIT OF HOLINESS indwelling in the Christian, when His purifying grace has its perfect work."

But Pope erects guards against including too much in our expectations. "Sin as generic," he says, "and belonging to the race in its federal constitution on earth, is not abolished till the time of which it is said, *Behold, I make all things new:* as something of the penalty remains untaken away, so also something of the peculiar concupiscence or liability to temptation or affinity with evil that besets man in this world remains. The saint delivered from personal sin is still connected with sin by his own past. . . we are numbered with the transgressors in one sense still, though not reckoned with them in another."[1]

Pope is reminding us that even though sanctified wholly we will have susceptibilities to sin and weaknesses of character which we would not have had if Adam had not sinned. We must therefore not presume that holiness means immunity to temptation, or that it guarantees impregnability of moral character. Only the person who is aware of his weak points and carefully guards them will retain the state of heart holiness for long.

Purity Defined

Now, having forestalled misconceptions by erecting these safeguards, it will be proper to attempt a definition of what is meant by heart purity. We can say first that initially it is a matter of cleansing from guilt and filthiness. This is the work of justification and regeneration. But the deeper cleansing includes also purging of the inner person from the remains of self- sovereignty. As a consequence there is governing the life a devotion to God that is undivided. As Kierkegaarde said, purity of heart is to "will one thing." To borrow the figure of an unknown Puritan, it is to have all the wheels of the soul turned the same direction. It is to be single-minded instead of double-minded. It is to be cured of the disposition to try to serve both God and mammon. It is to be filled with love and emptied of hate, bitterness, lust, and duplicity. It is for the outward profession to be matched by the inward preferences; for the basic drives and motives of the inner life to pass muster with God.

A Christian who is pure in heart has been cleansed of the selfish ambition of the disciples, the carnal envying and strife of the Corinthians, the greediness and deceit of Ananias and Sapphira, the love of power of Diotrephes, and the love of the world of Demas.

So much for the concept of heart purity, when seen against the backdrop of a biblical concept of carnality. But purity is not maturity, and to a consideration of that we turn next.

The Nature of Maturity

Whereas heart purity is an obtainment, maturity is an attainment. We may receive heart purity by the work of the Holy Spirit as a crisis experience, but we do not become mature that way. Maturity comes as the gradual fruition of a lot of living. Maturity to some modest degree, even in spiritual things, is the inevitable product of maturation—just naturally growing up. But maturity is also the product of battles fought, temptations resisted, obstacles overcome, problems solved, and wounds healed. Of one thing we may be sure: spiritual maturity is never reached without giving oneself to the spiritual life.

Maturity is relative. That is, we may today be more mature than we were when we started, but not as mature as we will be down the line. We may be more mature than some new Christians around us, but not yet as mature as some veteran saints we admire. However, as we walk with God, and learn the art of prayer warfare, and become familiar with the tutelage of the Spirit, we should within reasonable time reach a level of maturity which warrants some loads that immature Christians cannot safely carry.

Can we draw a profile of this level of maturity, at least partially? Maturity is both stability and depth. It is skill in living the Christian life. It includes discernment into people, movements, and doctrines. It is not easily fooled. It has in it poise in the midst of turmoil. It does not panic. It is so rooted and grounded in Christ, that it has some grasp of the length and breadth and depth and height of that love which passes understanding (Eph. 3:18). It is reasonable familiarity with the Scriptures and with the great cardinal doctrines of the faith. It is an adult love which has enlarged in its understanding and judgment, and is therefore able to discern things that matter (Phil. 1:9-10). It has worked out its salvation into consistent patterns of living and exemplary ethics (Phil. 2:12-14). A mature Christian understands himself and his fellows. He has come to terms with his own assignments and his own limitations. His feet are kept on the ground. A mature Christian is dependable. People know where he stands and where he will be, not only now but next week.

The Limitations of Maturity

But maturity is not flawlessness, nor is it a perfection of degree. No matter how relatively mature we may be, we are still striving earnestly to grow in grace and in the knowledge of the Lord (2 Pet. 3:18). We know with Paul that in many respects we have not arrived, or been "perfected" in the ultimate sense (Phil. 3:12). Therefore we need always to remind ourselves of Paul's reminder, that we "have this treasure in earthen vessels, that the surpassing greatness of the power may be of God and not from ourselves" (2 Cor. 4:7).

When Paul speaks of earthen vessels he means exactly what he says—vessels of clay, made out of the dust of the earth. This is a reference to all the propensities and limitations of our bodily existence. While the body is not sinful it is earthy, with its physical appetites and spatial and material groundings. But Paul has in mind not just the physical body as an organism but all the interactions of body and soul. We may be holy, but we are nevertheless beings pockmocked by sin and disease.

Therefore while the distinction between purity and maturity can be delineated to some degree, there are some fine lines which are more elusive. On the one hand there are sinners who have attained to an admirable level of maturity in the stability of their character and in the wholesomeness of their ethics; but it is a humanistic and self-achieved maturity which is built on pride rather than grace, and appears to be more than it actually is. On the other hand are Christians whose heart purity has not yet eliminated certain traits of immaturity which sometimes get in the way of a consistent Christian witness.

Some Special Problems of the Pure but Immature

We can say therefore that not only is sanctification not glorification, but sanctification does not mend all the cracks in the earthen vessels—at least not immediately or automatically. The pure but immature are often characterized by some special problems (especially the *very* immature!).

1. The pure but immature may still be marked by *strong appetites*, even perhaps some irregular appetites, not yet the subject of light, and therefore not yet condemnable. While temperance is a fruit of the Spirit, its application to our living habits may not immediately come into clear focus.

2. The pure but immature may bring some of their *crazy opinions* right along with them. Holiness does not make us infallible, though it will give us enough humility to discover the fact more quickly. The best proof of holiness is not being right always but being able to say, "I may be wrong." Opinions are the products of family training and community folklore, and they thrive especially well in the soil of ignorance. The problem is, the holders of wrong opinions do not know they are wrong. Therefore we need to be tolerant and patient with each other.

3. The pure but immature may be too limited in understanding and judgment to avoid *ethical blind spots*. One may be doing some things which are not completely consistent with holy living, without being aware of the fact. Some people

seem never to be quite capable of learning to think ethically at the fine print level. With these persons too we need to exercise tolerance and patience.

4. The pure but immature may suffer from *cultural impoverishment*. They may have deplorable tastes in music and art. They may be utterly devoid of any sense of propriety in dress. They may butcher "the King's English," be crude and boorish, loud-mouthed and tactless. But if truly filled with the Spirit, they will gradually respond to the better things. They may never learn correct grammar or acquire an appreciation for Handel's *Messiah*; but in many ways they will become gentle and refined. It may take years, but the Holy Spirit will either change them or leave them. For, as Oswald Chambers is quoted, "Slovenliness is an insult to the Holy Ghost."

5. The pure but immature may display *deficiencies in poise*. Only Jesus possessed perfect emotional poise in all situations. With us, relatively unflappable poise is a mark of *advanced* maturity, not fledgling. Some occasional displays of nervous irritability, depression, anxiety, or unwise obstinacy may crop up, which to the unsympathetic critic may look like carnality, but which may be rooted in nervous disorders, extreme fatigue, or perhaps the pressures of being loaded beyond our ability to cope. At other times physical or mental illness may be to blame. Here again the remedy—if a remedy is available in this life—is learning to live within our energy income. We must learn to trust, to draw on divine grace for the moment, to pace ourselves, to be realistic about our limitations, and above all, to live close to God in prayer and praise.

Sanctified Humanity and Its Parameters

How then can we describe the humanity of the sanctified? We can speak of it as original human nature, not now depraved by carnality, but still marred, and hence hindered by the infirmities and weaknesses which are indirect consequences of the Fall. On the one hand, while our humanity is still flawed and infirm, it is much more normal than is unregenerate and unsanctified humanity; yet on the other hand the restoration to normalcy is not yet complete. In spite of the frequent affirmation that it is, holiness is not instant *wholeness* in all facets of personhood.

It is time therefore to pinpoint certain aspects of human nature which relate to the joys and the problems of living a sanctified life. This will help us to understand the distinction between purity and maturity even more fully.

1. *The Christian experiences the complexity—and tension— of a nature that is at once spiritual and physical.* We are body, soul, and spirit (to use the trichotomy model, e.g., 1 Thess. 5:23). As *bodies* we are biological, sexual, and locational. We depend on food, water, and air for sustenance. We must have rest for renewal. We are earthbound and spacebound, confined to one place at a time, with limited fields of reach and awareness. In spite of what we used to think of our mothers, we don't have eyes in the back of our head. And we are continually in the process of dying.

As *souls* we are gregarious, creative, imaginative, inventive, acquisitive, inquisitive. The physical brain is the instrument or organ by which such mental processes are carried on, but the self controls the brain more than the brain controls the self.[2]

As *spirits* we are incurably religious and morally aware (we call this conscience). Because of the Fall, this side of our nature would be completely dormant if it were not for the partial recovery of prevenient grace and the quickening of the Holy Spirit.

It is popular these days to stress the unity of man's nature, and this prompts what is called the holistic approach to his problems. While it is true that the various components of man's being interact, they are not morally or spiritually equal. There are organic, psychosomatic, psychological, and spiritual illnesses, each pertaining to a distinct sphere of human nature. While they interrelate they are not indistinguishable, but clearly recognizable by competent persons, and must be treated according to the laws governing the nature of each. A sanctified person may still need to see the doctor, yes, in some cases, even the psychiatrist. There still may be the need for assistance in emotional and memory healing. While in a sense spiritual illness may overlap with physical, mental, and emotional illnesses, they are not qualitatively the same. In spiritual illness there is either sin or the threat of sin; furthermore, physical illness may be the consequence of sin; but in itself physical illness is morally neutral. Sickness is no proof of sin.

The tension between body and soul is inescapable therefore. Our aspirations outrun our physical capacities. We reach for the stars but our feet are stuck in the clay. Our performance does not match our intentions. To habitually be whipping oneself for such shortfall is the surest road to depression and breakdown, both physical and spiritual.

2. *Moreover, the Christian possesses a nature which unfolds under the laws of growth.* This has already been mentioned, but can be developed further at this point. Human life begins with conception, and moves through birth, childhood, adolescence, adulthood, and old age. There is in this sequence a maturation process which determines respective levels of capacity, understanding, and accountability. Spiritual life obeys the same laws of growth, from the new birth and entire sanctification through spiritual infancy, youth, and adulthood. In 1 John we have references to "dear children," "young men," and "fathers" (2:12-14). Whatever else this means, it at least is a suggestion that our spiritual growth bears some correspondence to our chronological growth. A sanctified adolescent will still be an adolescent.

3. *Next, we need to be reminded that human nature, even though sanctified, remains under the sentence of death.* It is this which determines the fact that growth and maturity in the

natural order will give way to old age and its inevitable demise. But it is this also which determines that this process will be marked by disease, pain, and numerous abnormalities. Mental illnesses, such as Alzheimer's; diseases of the nervous system, such as Parkinson's and other wasting diseases; and various forms of physical breakdowns, are the common lot of humanity, and the sanctified Christian is not guaranteed exemption. Yet each form of progressive death has some degree of power to distort the personality, and even the behavior. The behavior of an old person being destroyed by arteriosclerosis is not necessarily indicative of the real person, and may not be a proof of carnality.

4. *Again, the sanctified Christian as well as others possesses a nature which is normatively social.* He belongs in a specific culture. He is the product of a family, a community, a nation, an ethos, and a race. Every facet of his environment and lineage leaves its stamp on him. The sanctified Eskimo may have characteristics not found in sanctified Americans, or Japanese, or Africans. Moreover, it is this societal trait in human nature (as well as sexuality) which prompts marriage and the family, and which creates friendships and alliances, whether political, commercial, or personal. Neighborhood towns, and cities, are held together by man's gregarious nature.

This also underlies the church. While the bond between Christians is first of all spiritual, and thus on a higher level than mere gregariousness, it nevertheless has an element of simple sociability in it. Becoming a hermit therefore is both unbiblical and unnatural. A lively social life is not incompatible with holiness—provided we pray together as well as play together.

5. *A yet further aspect of human nature which is as normal to the sanctified as to the unsanctified is the fact of unique individuality.* While gregarious, we are yet private. We share in common a *basic* human nature, yet each is an unre-

peatable individual, with traits and capacities all our own. Holiness does not change this. Sanctified people are not clones (though sometimes we have tried hard to make ourselves clones!). While this individuality makes for richness in human relationships, it also provides occasion for stress, incompatibility, and misunderstanding. Holiness may give the disposition to want to communicate and relate and adjust in love, but it does not automatically eliminate the need for much grace, at times, in the process.

6. A reminder may be timely here: No matter what the degree of maturity, we are still human, and *humanity is both fallible and finite*. Not only do we remain circumscribed by physical limitations, but mental as well. This means that holiness does not guarantee perfection of judgment, and sanctified people can get themselves into jams that "you wouldn't believe." I am not now thinking of the times when we suffer from the stupidity of others, but the times when we suffer from our own. As members of a fallen race, living under the curse in the natural order, it is to be expected that we should share the calamities that are the common lot of man. But sometimes we may miscalculate or misjudge a person or situation and bring upon ourselves financial reverses, social debacles and domestic agonies which crush the spirit and prompt anguished cries to God. If we don't believe, for instance, that holy people can marry unwisely, we need only point to John Wesley. But the difference between holy people and unholy is the reassuring presence of the Holy Spirit, the humility which seeks for God's way out (or *through*), and the trust which like Job refuses to charge "God foolishly" (Job 11:22).

Holiness and the Self

Some clarification is needed also in understanding the nature of the ego or self, and the effect of heart cleansing upon it. This is the nucleus, or core, of personal identity, around which the infinite variations of personal individuality cluster.

For this ego to be crucified with Christ does not mean its extinction; that would be the end of the person. It means for the ego to be dead to its carnal claim to autonomy. A crucified self never says, "I want it my way," and it is rid of the disposition to demand one's own happiness and claim one's own rights without regard either to God or to man. A sanctified self is a subordinate self, and it is a tamed self. This is the meaning of having the meekness and humility of Christ (Matt. 11:28-30).

But while the sanctified self is cleansed of excessive egoism, and it is no longer self-centered before God, it is still a powerful entity with inalienable propensities. These propensities must forever be guarded, lest there be a reversion to carnal-mindedness.

What are these propensities which need to be guarded, lest they get out of hand?

1. For one thing, *it is natural for the self to be self-protective*; which gives rise to the defensiveness of insecurity. Yet a sick self-protectiveness is on the very edge of a sinful self-centeredness. There is a very fine line here. The Holy Spirit will help us surrender our ego for bruising. He will teach us to avoid the touchiness of supersensitivity.

2. It is natural for *the self to be in some degree combative*, in the sense of an impulse to solve problems and overcome difficulties; and also in the sense of a capacity for confrontation when questions of right and wrong are at stake. Yet this combativeness, if not checked and controlled by the Spirit, can become pugnaciousness, even pigheadedness. Becoming mature includes the discovery that we don't have to fix everything—or everybody.

3. Then, even still more basic, it is natural for the self to "prefer success to failure, praise to blame, being understood to being misunderstood, health to illness, pleasure to pain, freedom of movement to being bound (Acts 26:29), comfortable circumstances to pinching poverty."[3] And we can appropriately

add—being loved rather than being hated. But in these respects, too, self must be kept on the cross, for at times it will be very easy to come down, and seek to escape its pain and rugged demands.

Summary

What then is sanctified human nature like?[4] It is essentially the same kind of nature which is shared by all human beings. This nature is both fixed and malleable. In its biological and physiological aspects it is unchangeable until the resurrection. It is subject to all the natural laws governing this planet—gravitation, night and day, seasons, growth processes, and time. On the other hand, in its spiritual and moral aspects it is subject to change. An evil nature may become good; a good nature may become evil. While human nature is "locked in" in some respects it is alterable in others. This malleability is endemic to human nature, per se, as divinely created.

Sanctified human nature is still finite, and therefore still fallible. It is susceptible to misjudgments and miscalculations. It groans in pain, bleeds when cut, agonizes in sorrow. It has profound needs—needs for love, acceptance, belonging; and also for achievement. It has unbelievable capacities for creativity, for adaptation, and for growth. It desires to marry and have children. It becomes attached to people and places. It bears traits from unique blood lines as well as traits of race and culture.

Sanctified human nature is no different from unsanctified in the basic processes of human life. It is subject to weariness, pain, disease, and death. If it is to function normally the brain and body must be reasonably healthy. It must labor if it would possess. It must study if it would become knowledgeable. It must think if it would understand. Invisible realities are still opaque; i.e., they are not immediately open to sight and experience, but must be mediated by secondary agencies. These agencies are angels, the Bible and the Holy Spirit. The Holy Spirit has given us the Word and illumines our minds in understanding it. But even with the Spirit's aid, sanctified human nature is still terrestrial, not yet celestial.

But this sanctified human nature also bears the scars which mark a race which has degenerated physically and mentally by a history of sin. These scars in the sanctified take multiple forms—temperamental imbalance; a broad spectrum of intelligence spread; special susceptibilities which spell weaknesses requiring life-long watching; personal idiosyncrasies which may make their possessor difficult to understand or even live with.

Sanctified human nature, therefore, will not be wholly normal, as it would be if sin had not entered the human stream. But it will be relatively normal, at least far more so than the nature of the unregenerated and unsanctified. For now it will be a three-dimensional being instead of two. Without God human nature is abridged, unable to function in all its created capacities; as such it is both abnormal and subnormal. But human nature finds its center and therefore its essential normalcy when pervaded by the Holy Spirit. It is more normal than before its Pentecost because now freed from the warp and twist of the carnal mind. It is open to God. Because delivered from its alienation toward God and restored to the full functioning of its spiritual self, through the infilling with the Spirit, sanctified human nature pulsates with the energy of divine love.

Earlier we made reference to Paul's reminder that "we have this treasure in earthen vessels" (2 Cor. 4:7). Through most of the chapter we have focused on the earthiness of these vessels, even after entire sanctification. This has been necessary lest we confuse holiness with an unrealistic and impossible ideal.

But in our attention to the earthiness of the vessel we should not lose sight of the "treasure" within the vessel. Paul has just delineated it: "But God, who said, 'Light shall shine out of darkness,' is the One who has shone in our hearts to give the light of the knowledge of the glory of God in the face of Jesus Christ" (v. 5). In the vessel is a shining light. It is the revelation of God in Christ, mediated to us by the Holy Spirit. It is the indwelling Christ. Because God has in His triune personhood made His home within us, He is in the process of making us more and more like himself. He is establishing within us the "mind of Christ" (Phil. 2:5, KJV). There has been "poured out within our hearts" the love of God "through the Holy spirit who was given to us" (Rom. 5:5). In Christ we have all the resources of heaven at our faith-tips for living a holy and victorious life, in spite of the earthiness of the vessel.

While the earthiness of the vessel has not been removed, all filthiness has. It is a clean vessel. Moreover, the treasure within imparts newness to the very nature of the vessel.

That which is the peculiar glory of this newness is the spontaneous affinity of sanctified human nature for God and holy things. This affinity is not spasmodic but the normal response of the entire being. What before was a matter of striving, because of the drag of indwelling sin, has now become perfectly natural. Sanctified human nature is no longer at war with itself. It is no longer a multiple or divided nature. The whole being gravitates toward God. In being at home with God it is at home with itself.

Let us then by all means let God consummate His complete sanctifying work within us, until we are spiritually at home. Then let us "work out" our salvation in daily life "with fear and trembling" (Phil. 2:12), in the sense of reverent carefulness. And let us help God answer Paul's prayer for us that our "love may abound more and more in knowledge and in all judgment; That [we] may approve things that are excellent; that [we] may be sincere and without offence till the day of Christ" (Phil. 1:9-10, KJV).

ENDNOTES

1. *A Compendium of Christian Theology* (London: Wesleyan Conference Office, 1880), Vol. III, p. 47.

2. See my article "The Relation of the Holy Spirit to the Self," *Wesleyan Theological Journal*, Fall, 1987 (Vol. 22, No. 2), p. 84. I discuss also the place of the brain in this relationship.

3. Quoted from *Exploring Christian Holiness*, Vol. III, "The Theological Formulation," p. 219.

4. I am aware that I am going against the tide *in some circles* by talking about "nature." The term is an offense to behaviorists in psychology and existentialists in philosophy and theology, who tend to eschew metaphysics. Such ideologies stress individual being rather than generic, and would rather talk about personal natures than generic human nature. Rejected especially is the Platonic concept of a prior *idea* of human nature which is more real than the individualized experience of it, i.e., an abstract "nature" which underlies all concrete human natures. But we don't have to be Platonists to realize that the concept of nature cannot be exorcised from rational thought. If we define it as "the essence or essential character of something" (*Baker's Pocket Dictionary of Religious Terms*), we see "nature" as the necessary corollary of "race." Every person is bound to every other human being by sharing in a common ancestry and sharing in common indispensable characteristics which make it possible to affirm humanness. Every person participates in a unique nature of humanness which distinguishes humanness from the nature of dogs, flowers, or rocks. And running through racial nature, because of the Fall, are negative tendencies, which prompt Paul to declare that all of us (apart from grace) are "by nature objects of wrath" (Eph. 2:3, NIV). And redemption reaches not only the ego but the nature too. Whereas we were by nature objects of wrath we can become by nature sharers of God's holiness (2 Pet. 1:3-4).

Works Cited

Byrum, Russell. *Christian Theology*. Anderson, IN: Warner Press, rev., 1982 (Original, 1925). Revision ed. Arlo F. Newell.

Chapman, James B. *Holiness, the Heart of Christian Experience*. Kansas City, MO: Nazarene Publishing House, 1943.

Dawson, Grace. *Set Among Princes*. Kansas City, MO: Beacon Hill Press of Kansas City, 1979.

Dayton, Wilber. "The Acts," *The Wesleyan Biblical Commentary*, vol. 5. Grand Rapids: William B. Eerdmans Publishing Company, 1965. General Editor, Charles W. Carter.

Dunning, Ray. *Grace, Faith, and Holiness*. Kansas City, MO: Beacon Hill Press of Kansas City, 1988.

Earle, Ralph. "The Acts," *Beacon Bible Commentary*, vol. VII. General Editor, Albert Harper. Kansas City, MO: Beacon Hill Press, 1965.

Kauffman, Donald T., ed. *Baker's Pocket Dictionary of Religious Terms*. Grand Rapids: Baker Book House, repr. 1975; orig. 1967.

Kromminga, Carl G. "Temptation," *Baker's Dictionary of Theology*. Editor-in-Chief, Everett F. Harrison. Grand Rapids: Baker Book House, 1960.

Ockenga, Harold John. *Power Through Pentecost*. Grand Rapids: Wm. B. Eerdmans Publishing Company, 1959.

Oesterley, W.E. "The General Epistles of James," *The Expositor's Greek Testament*, vol. 4. Gen. editor, W. Robertson Nicoll. Grand Rapids: Wm. B. Eerdmans Publishing Company, 1967.

Pope, William Burt. *A Compendium of Christian Theology*. London: Wesleyan Conference Office, 1880.

Purkiser, W.T. *Exploring Christian Holiness*, vol. 1, "The Biblical Foundations." Kansas City, MO: Beacon Hill Press of Kansas City, 1983.

Robertson, A.T. *Word Pictures in the New Testament.* New York: Harper & Brothers, Publishers, 1931.

Steele, Daniel. *Mile-stone Papers.* Minneapolis, MN: Bethany Fellowship, reprint, nd; originally 1878.

—*Half-Hours With St. Paul.* Boston Christian Witness Co., 1894.

Taylor, Richard S. *Great Holiness Classics*, vol. 3, "Leading Wesleyan Thinkers." Kansas City, MO: Beacon Hill Press of Kansas City, 1985.

—*Exploring Christian Holiness*, vol. 3, "The Theological Formulation." Kansas City, MO: Beacon Hill Press of Kansas City, 1985.

—"The Relation of the Holy Spirit to the Self," *Wesleyan Theological Journal,* Fall, 1987 (Vol. 22, No. 2).

Thayer, Joseph Henry. *Greek-English Lexicon of the New Testament.* Grand Rapids: Zondervan, 1963.

Turner, George. *The Vision Which Transforms.* Kansas City, MO: Beacon Hill Press, 1964.

Watson, William. "Temptation, Trial," *Dictionary of the Apostolic Church,* vol. 2. Ed. by James Hastings. Grand Rapids: Baker Book House, 1973.

Wesley, John. *The Works of John Wesley*, vols. 5, 6, 11. Kansas City: Nazarene Publishing House, as a reprint of the authorized edition published by the Wesleyan Conference Office in London, England, in 1872.

Wiley, H. Orton. *Christian Theology*, vol. 2. Kansas City, MO: Nazarene Publishing House, 1941.

Williams Charles B. *The New Testament: A Translation in the Language of the People.* Chicago: Moody Bible Institute, 1937, 1965.

Wood, Laurence. *Pentecostal Grace.* Wilmore, KY: Francis Asbury Publishing Company, Inc., 1980.